The
Fullness
of
Life

Paul Kurtz / The

Fullness

of

Life

Horizon Press   New York

Library of Congress Cataloging in Publication Data
Kurtz, Paul W.
   The fullness of life.

   1. Humanism—20th century. 2 Humanistic ethics.
3. World politics—1945—   I. Title.
B821.K84   191   74-11176
ISBN 0-8180-1318-4
ISBN 0-8180-1320-6 (pbk.)

Manufactured in the United States of America

Contents

The
Fullness
of
Life

Preface

CRISIS HUMANOLOGY

Can human beings live without religion? Theistic religions, which profess belief in God, are now in retreat. Most traditional moral and philosophical guideposts seem to be crumbling. Indeed, it is difficult for people to accept the old virtues. Many individuals are lost and alone in a world of narrowing options. Are there new directions to be taken?

The present moment is unique on the scale of human time, for many conflicting tendencies are unfolding in rapid pace. The alternatives are critical: On the one hand, we have increased our power to fulfill our visions of the good, to expand our horizons of creativity and progress; on the other, we can squander this great opportunity and allow the fruits of our efforts to dissipate. Prometheus stole the arts and fire from the gods, and with these he built civiliza-

9

tion. Promethean humans are now unbound and prepared for further massive leaps into space; we have the capability to colonize the universe, to alter our environment radically, control our behavior, and guide our evolution in daring directions. But Promethean humans— by their failure to act, by ignorance or cowardice, or misdirected passion—can topple the fragile edifice of civilization and perhaps end in an apocalyptic immolation, appropriate to the kind of heroic figures that we have become.

The dilemma is pressing, pregnant with rich possibility or tragic defeat. Modern man, in abandoning the dehumanizing beliefs of the infancy of the race and in replacing the former dependence upon a divine universe with new confidence, can now modify the world to fit his needs and use reason and science, in technology, morality, and political organization, to build a better life. Illusions to the contrary, the human species now stands alone, without benefit of a mythology to bolster it. Can we summon the courage to continue to develop new modes of existence or will other forms of religion, vain, deluding, and suicidal, again overwhelm us?

This is the century of greatest danger and promise. It can become the century of humanism; it is the time in which large sections of the educated classes have become aware of the true character of the human enterprise; they have come to realize that we are on our own, that the religious faiths of bygone ages can no longer help us, that we are responsible for our future.

Nietzsche heralded the recognition that God is dead and that man must live for himself. But if the symbols and ideals of an earlier supernatural tradition are no longer relevant, what can replace them? Must humans embrace new and more virulent ideological religions of intensity and commitment? Will Marxism, of which so many modern intellectuals are enamored, become the dominant religion? Or can human beings create more appropriate symbols and ideals? If God is dead, will man be able to thrive? The crisis we face is a *crisis humanology*: it concerns the destiny and the possible death of man.

We can still destroy ourselves in nuclear or bio-chemical warfare; we can by technological blight so poison our environment, and we can so increase our population that it will be impossible for humans to live decently. Alternatively we can participate in creating a better future, free of religious mythology, by using technology for the betterment of humankind and using reason to develop a moral revolution in human conduct. A moral revolution, which is just beginning to emerge, would involve a fundamental restructuring of our ideals and values. It would encourage us to discover and achieve the fullness of life, to create a society in which individuals are liberated from the tyranny of unnecessary legal and social restraints, a society in which there is genuine toleration for diverse life styles, and in which equality and democratic participation are guiding principles. If human beings are to achieve these ends, however, they can do so only by attempting to ameliorate conditions on a global scale. This means, for example, that we must create institutions of a world community and that we must engage in world-wide economic, ecological, and technological planning.

The challenge to post-modern man is to reaffirm life, to learn to face the future with courage and audacity. We must ask the questions anew, Who are we? What are we capable of? Are we willing to create a new tomorrow for ourselves, and indeed for the whole of humankind?

—Paul Kurtz
Amherst, New York

Part One / Anti-Anti-Humanisms

I / The End of Theism

THE GOD IDEA

Some will say that, since God is dead for contemporary man, it is not necessary to beat on the coffin of supernaturalism. Intellectuals and sophisticated educated people at least no longer believe in divine providence or immortality. The churches are everywhere in disarray. What need again to debunk the existence of God for an age that has lost faith in him?

The reason is, simply, that God has died many times before: in classical Greece, during the Renaissance, in the Enlightenment, and in the 19th century. Yet, however dead in one age, the idea returns, haunting man by its attraction and taunting him with its mystery. There are many surrogates for classical religion—nationalism, patriotism, technocracy, scientism, utopianism; and new cults of unreason are ever ready to intervene. For many men the God idea of the priest has been transformed into the utopian vision of the commissar. Catholicism has in some measure been replaced by Marxism-Leninism; both are institutionalized religions. So religious mythology has not been fully overthrown. It has its roots in cultural lag and institutional drift. Some traditions die hard; though a living belief may be refuted in one period, hollow forms remain and new forms of the faith may emerge in the next. The God idea, then, is difficult to weed out permanently, because it is rooted in human fear, and nourished by human hope—two passions that are perennial in the breast of man. To deal with it we must resist the dread and horror of the unknown and provide a positive sense of the anticipation of the good. We must use critical reason as our major therapy. Yet in dealing with irrational fears and vain hopes, this is not enough; these mortal passions must be profoundly rerooted in new ground.

The originative source of the God idea is man facing the problem of death and his quest for the meaning of life. How shall a man, especially a free man, aware of the changing character of nature and sensitive to the end of his mortal existence, deal with death? In the face of my extinction, how can I build a meaningful life?

Theistic religion has its original source in eschatology. It begins with the awesome recognition that all things within nature come into existence and pass away, that human life is transient and ephemeral. It is the feeble effort of man to cope with the apparent finality of death: my death, the death of my loved one, the end of my deepest longings and values, the destruction of my dreams and those of my civilization. Sir James Frazer maintains in *The Golden Bough* that fearful abhorrence of the dead is, on the whole, the most powerful stimulus of primitive religion; and Bronislaw Malinowski holds in *Magic, Science, and Religion* that the individual's anxiety and the fear of his own death have been the source of religious piety and awe. These accounts surely do not exhaust all of the origins of religion; yet they point to an enduring source of religious belief. Stonehenge and the Pyramids are testimonies of men's efforts to stave off the inevitable; the World Trade Center towers and the Kremlin have the same fate in store for them. Every human being, whether Alexander or Aristotle, Jesus or Shakespeare, Tolstoy or Marx, has had to face the same existentialist dilemma.

Theism, as indicated above, is an effort to plumb the depths of the mystery and pathos of death. What is the origin of my life? "Why should there be something rather than nothing?" asks Heidegger. Man, rooted in being, faces nonbeing, and he seeks an explanation. He needs to know why his existence is inevitably so fragile, and reads into nature his longing and desire for a ground for human existence, and for the purpose or goal of his existence. For the religious believer, nothingness is denied by eternal being, and a ground and source of being sustains all that is and will be.

EFFORTS TO DEMONSTRATE GOD'S EXISTENCE

Belief in God, then, basically has a psychological source, even though there have been many attempts in the history of thought to "prove" the existence of God. The so-called cosmological argument is familiar; many of the best minds have been attracted by its seductive logic. Beginning with any observed event, there is an effort to "explain" its rootedness in ultimate being. No event, it is argued, can be uncaused, or the cause of itself, but must be caused by another. But if so, it is argued, the cause of an observed event must itself be an effect; thus, it too must have a cause; and so on. We may thus theoretically trace causes further back. But how far? An infinite regress of causes is a paradox, we are told; hence, there must be a First Cause, itself uncaused, the eternal cause of all events, pure or actual Being itself.

Philosophers have exposed the curious contradictions in this tortuous logic: Why assume that causes are real entities in nature, rather than convenient explanatory devices invented by us; why assume that series of causal explanations are interrelated rather than plural; why reject an infinite regress or infinite past; if everything must have a cause, then is it not a contradiction to postulate an uncaused cause, because the mind will not accept infinite mysteries and unknowables?

The theist cannot accept chance or misadventure in nature or the fact that human beings have no special roots in an eternal being: This would be an unfathomable mystery, making the universe "unintelligible." So he postulates an omniscient and omnipotent being who is infinite and mysterious; in so doing, however, he has only pushed our ignorance back one step. For we can always ask: What is the cause of the first cause?—a question often said by believers to be illegitimate. But the unbeliever replies that if this question is illegitimate, so is the whole line of reasoning that led to it. What cognitive significance does the inquiry into first causes have? The answer is clear: The cosmological quest is dubious on methodological grounds; it provides no basis for evidential confirmation.

To talk about cause and effect in the observed world and in the sciences—a flash flood caused by a storm, a disease caused by spores —is to deal with the world of observables; and we can confirm our hypothesis by tests. To talk about an uncaused cause is to transcend the categories of experience. Causal explanations are conditional hypotheses: We say, whenever a occurs, b will follow; a has occurred, therefore b; thus a probably is the cause of b. But to adduce an alleged divine cause is a misuse of language; for the cause is unconditional and resists experimental verification. The theologian who claims to find satisfaction in the cosmological proof has only assumed what he has set out to prove, reinstated what he already believed. The cosmological argument is not an argument so much as a surrogate for a need: the profound human tendency to be rooted, to seek parentage, to feel secure.

Yet it is not the quest for beginnings that is the real source of theism, but the quest for a future, the need for a purpose. Man has a curious interest in history, a fascination for things past; but he has a greater need for the future. He asks not simply, where did I come from, but where will I end up?

The classical teleological argument for the existence of God thus has special attraction and appeal in dealing with the puzzlement of existence; for it is an attempt to read purpose into nature. If the individual cannot find any final purpose in his mortal existence, he invests the universe with a purpose larger than his own, one that is divine and eternal. Here hope and promise serve to assuage fear and trembling, in the face of death and the tragic. To live is to encounter problems, insecurity, dangers. Life is precarious. The unexpected occurs. The awful ensues: disease, plague, war, accident, the bizarre, death. Man learns that he is more clever than most animals; there are things he can do that they cannot. Yet there seem to be things beyond his control, powers in the universe greater than he; powers unpredictable and mysterious. He then attempts to put himself into a proper relationship with those powers; and tribal religions dramatize his response. He performs ceremony and prayer to supplicate the unknown; his ritual is a purgative to cleanse his fear and a means to influence, if he can, his future. He feels utterly dependent. He asks, How shall I face these contingencies? Where shall I get the strength to exist in the face of adversity?

Here the God-myth enters and offers some security and guarantee that while all's not well now, all will be well in the end, if only man will have faith in the eternal future. For human animals to read into nature their frailties and powers is, after all, all too human. God himself is man deified, the father endowed with superhuman strength, the creative source, the grand ejaculator who spews his semen into the womb and sustains it, not temporarily but forever. If lions had Gods, said Xenophon, they would be lion-like in nature. And so God is man transformed, and divine cosmology is a humanology constructed in grand style. The immortality fable develops: Eternal blessedness will finally sustain those who are unflinching and undoubting; the dead will achieve peace and serenity.

This is not intended as a historical reconstruction of the derivation of religion, which has multiple origins, complex forms, and many roles. What I am interested in focusing on is the function that religion performs in human civilization, particularly its psychological function. The many functions that religion has, including roles in maintaining social solidarity, may be described and explained naturalistically. There is no mystery in religion; the mystery only lies in what religions claim to be about. Religion is a form of human behavior, an expression of belief and sentiment. It attempts to satisfy a deep-felt need: it grows out of man's feelings of impotence, his dependence, his need for assurance and consolation concerning his origins and his future.

Concern about the future is the chief source of the religious impulse. A belief in divinity becomes a belief in teleology—in the doctrine that there are hidden intentions and deeper prospects than our mortal life can fulfill. Indeed, the teleological argument, claiming to discover divine purpose in existence, has been offered by theologians as still another "proof" of divine existence. Everywhere around us, says the theist, we see order and pattern. Things come into existence and pass away in terms of causal law; although there seem to be change and contingency, this is only apparent; underlying it all there is a basic reason and order. Order must imply design; and this means there is a plan or purpose in nature. How can there be design without a divine designer? it is asked. Therefore God must surely exist.

This argument from design is fallacious. For the discovery of "order" in nature may be the order that we impose upon the world. Along with "order" we encounter "disorder" and conflict, which we cannot easily explain away. Human frailty imposes an order and form upon the universe, one that is comfortable and satisfying to man. In any case, even if there were an underlying order to nature this does not justify the inference that there is a design or a designer. The teleological argument was introduced in a pre-Darwinian era; nature has no "purposes" is the conclusion of modern science.

Some theists have nevertheless attempted a teleological interpretation of evolution. Yet evolution surely does not allow us to read vital entelechies into nature. Processes of natural selection, adaptation, or mutation do not imply design. Nor should we assume that man is the end of history or its highest manifestation, particularly since life probably exists in other star systems. The course of human history is open, it is a function of many factors, none of them fixed. Although events may in principle at least be explained causally, this does not mean they are divinely pre-ordained.

The lonely individual wants to believe that the future is preordained, that somehow there will be a place for him in the scheme of things, that the beauty of life and the joy of love, friendship and kindness, sweetness and pleasure, will not be lost forever; and that his fear and foreboding of death are without foundation. The God idea thus appeals as an ideal. It has profound moral dimensions; for it attempts to give meaning and direction to his anxiety-ridden life. But the teleological argument is without empirical foundation and rests on wish-fulfillment.

There are those who nevertheless persist in the belief that there are two realms, the "knowable" and the "unknowable." The "knowable" world of ordinary experience can be sensed and understood by observation and reason, it is said, but the "unknowable" realm cannot be approached this way. We may, however, get a fleeting glimmer of its presence and of a power "of which none greater can be conceived." Thus religious faith is often nourished by a mystical reverence for the source of our being that transcends our understanding.

Primitive man in ignorance and fear sensed that there were obscure forces and hidden powers which he could not control. He was unaware that bacteria caused disease, that genetic interchange was responsible for acquired characteristics, and that disturbances within the earth's core led to volcanic eruptions. Who else but the gods were responsible? Man now recognizes the fact that there are naturalistic causal explanations that can be given for these formerly inexplicable events. Nevertheless, some poets and prophets find life richer than logic, and feeling deeper than sense perception; and so by intuition they seek to plumb depths unexplored.

There is no denying the existence of profound "spiritual" passions, of deep-felt longings and sensations. But that these are signs of another reality is, of course, purely conjectural, and that they involve knowledge which we cannot discover any other way is doubtful. To know something is to be able to relate it to other portions of our experience. But to know something about the world, to attribute properties and characteristics to it, suggests that we must be able to test our hunches by some experimental refinement. The mystic cannot do this. His premonitions, like hallucinatory experiences, exist within his psychological world, but that they designate or refer to some external reality independent of him is a claim that must be judged with critical care. The mystical claim of a revelatory truth tells us little about the universe; on the other hand it tells us much about man, about his language and aspirations, wishes and fantasies, needs and desires.

RELIGION AND MORALITY

This suggests the double character of human existence; for mysticism is fixated in a quest for values. Man lives in two worlds: the worlds of passion and fear, of hope and despair, of joy and sorrow. It is in the tension between the actual world in which we must endure and the ideal world we strive for that the mystic's wishes are fulfilled in his visions. For the mystic longs for and discovers, underneath the imperfect world of insecurity and flux, a perfect world of security and peace. God is all good, the fountain of perfection; and the glimmer of a realm seen only dimly is his hope that there is a better universe in which beauty and justice prevail.

Mysticism fails as a method of establishing a divine presence. It does not reveal an underlying ultimate truth about reality, but rather points to an underlying craving of human beings. Religion, whether as primitive worship of unknown animistic forces, or in its more sophisticated form as mystical revelation, points to a common fact about man. It is an effort to provide support for belief and sentiment. In its most profound function, therefore, it is *moral*. It offers hope and direction to a confused mind in the face of insecurity, adversity, death. It gives man courage to go on.

The affinity of religion and morality is much deeper than this. Given the basic moral thrust, the sense of meaning given to human existence, religion then intervenes in all aspects of life. It becomes institutionalized, supported by tradition and law, codified and ritualized. A priestly class emerges, most often tied to the dominant economic or political powers within society. The priests impose the moral law upon all phases of human behavior, including sexual relations ("Thou shalt not commit adultery"), economic relations ("Thou shalt not steal") and social relations, as in the family ("Honor thy father and thy mother").

Theistic religion at first offers balm to the frightened spirit seeking support. In the process, however, it is often transformed into a source of repression of human personality. The commitment to a moral ideal as the guarantee of salvation is supplanted by commitment to the church; and eventually church traditions and the institutionalized hierarchy that interprets it may become more important than the original message.

There are three stages in the development of a religion: the simple message enunciated as a source of hope, the gradual institutionalization and organization of its code as a way of life, and its eventual corruption and decay.

This does not deny that there have been positive moral attributes cultivated by the theistic way of life. At its finest, Christianity has preached an ethic of love and sympathy toward all men, it has often provided the motive for altruism and the inspiration for the creative arts and poetry. If the brotherhood of man under the fatherhood of God exists, then we owe a debt to our fellow creatures. The virtues of kindness, honesty, and charity have helped to tame the wild human beast and make him sociable.

"SINS" AGAINST MAN

Yet at the same time that the human animal was domesticated, his natural talents were denigrated. Theism has left a sad legacy of "sins" to man. The first, no doubt, has been the tendency to suppress truth. Until very recent times, theism has consistently made war against certain forms of humanistic philosophy and science. Theology has attempted to exploit philosophy or destroy its critical process. And there has been in response a long and hard battle waged by freethinkers, from Socrates to Bruno and Galileo, to defend the right to free inquiry. Theism has tended to extirpate heresy, condemn deviationism, banish revisionism. It was only with the Renaissance and the beginning of modern science that toleration was enunciated and eventually came to prevail.

Authoritarian religion is on the defensive in the modern world. It has been difficult for it to withstand the application of the scientific method to nature, man, and society. Yet there is always the danger that dogma and creed will again prevail and that a bureaucratized and institutionalized church will again seek to impose an absolutistic version of the truth. Fortunately, the history of mankind demonstrates the difficulty in defining a fixed body of "perennial truths." Doubts emerge, the creative mind of man breaks forth, old systems decay and are destroyed. The method of authority, as Charles Peirce observed, is unable to hold the line against new ideas. It is fear of critical questioning that prompts authoritarianism to try to stamp out new ideas and daring visions of the truth. Critical intelligence is thus the main enemy of the orthodox theologian whose natural tendency is to prohibit truth from entering the "spiritual realm."

Authoritarianism, at least in its most extreme form, has often been wedded to fanaticism, unquenchable faith in a rigid doctrine of salvation. The chief virtue for a fanatic is obedience and submission to the Word. The true believer can brook no compromise with his first principles, which are taken as axiomatic truths. While others may waver in their faith, he seeks to hold fast. Tenacity is one of the highest virtues of the believer, the true test of whether he shall enter the gates of heaven.

Accordingly, coupled with this there is an intolerance of other faiths and beliefs. The tragic paradox of religious faith is the tendency of its noble ideals to be perverted by ignoble servitude. Insofar as religion binds man to a set of attitudes, to a way of life, to forms of ceremony and ritual, it closes him to adventure; he cannot appreciate other similar claims. His alone is the genuine message. Religions thus held have degenerated into warring sects, marked off by walls of intolerance. Love for God and man is easily converted to intolerant hatred for other tribes and communities. Thus the narrow religious frame has often imposed inflexibility as the proper response to criticism and disagreement. It is insensitive to the doubt and indeterminacy that are inevitable in any inquiry that attempts to be honest. Perhaps it is unfair to indict the original religious impulse for all the mistakes that ensue in its name. Yet it is precisely the fear of the unknown and the hunger for certainty in a quixotic world that finally leads the believer to a shore where he can stand firm against opposition to his faith and insensitive to contradictions in his beliefs. Out of this psychological propensity is born the authoritarian personality, which feeds on intolerance.

A second "sin" that theism has committed against man has been its perverted view of the human body. Not all forms of theism have been so corrupted. Yet there has been a constant theme—from the doctrine of original sin in Paul and Augustine down through Catholicism and Puritanism—which maintains that the body is impure and debased, and that sex is evil, not to be enjoyed but controlled and suppressed. The fact that the Church has exalted celibacy and chastity is a sign of its pathology. Indeed, the continual denial of active biological impulses and needs may very well be the Church's worst offense against humanity. How much anguish and suffering has this distorted view of human nature caused? To insist that sex is wicked and merely to be endured and that the primary purpose of sexuality is reproduction within marriage, not enjoyment, is antihumanistic. Sexual enjoyment, exploration, and excitement can be beautiful sources of experience. Yet we have inherited a doctrine that breeds guilt and weighs people down with conflict. Claiming to provide existential peace and security, theism has only exacerbated insecurity by attempting to corrode innocent human passions.

The pathology of theism is compounded not only by its distorted sense of "moral turpitude" but by the threat of divine sanction in imposing its pathology and institutionalizing its code by means of law. Repressive theism has inculcated a depraved view of sexuality. Incalculable suffering has been engendered by phobias against contraception, abortion, adultery, and divorce. An extreme male chauvinism has been perpetrated in the name of Biblical authority. The double standard in Western civilization originated with the Hebrews: The Old Testament permits a man sexual pleasures denied to a woman, who was expected to be a virgin at marriage and faithful thereafter. Paul in the New Testament admonishes wives to submit themselves to their husbands, "For the husband is the head of the wife, even as Christ is the head of the Church . . . Therefore as the Church is subject unto Christ, so let the wives be subject to their own husbands in everything" (*Ephesians*, 5). Thus women have been mastered by men in the sanctity of monogamous marriage. Similar repression has been levelled against homosexuals and lesbians; their sexuality likewise condemned as bestial. If there were no other achievement in the 20th century, its greatest advance would be its liberation from sexual repression. Humanism has set the stage for human beings to rediscover their genitals as a source of happiness and enrichment without guilt or fear.

The third "sin" of theism is its attempt to deflect concern from this life to the afterlife; in doing this it has often allied itself with the status quo and vested interests against social change and reconstruction. Religionists have often rationalized social, economic, political, and racial injustices. The battle for the extension of democracy, liberty, and equality has until recent times advanced in spite of opposition by the churches. The priestly classes have often allied themselves with oppressive oligarchies, opposed to the extension of elementary human rights to others. They have obstructed the application of critical intelligence to the solution of social and moral problems, as they have obstructed its full application to theological questions. The narrowness of this may be seen in the Roman Catholic Church's opposition to effective birth control. At a time when the population explosion is a major social concern, the Church continues to resist sorely needed measures for contraception, sterilization, and abortion. It would, it seems, suffer poverty, disease, and gratuitous death as results of excessive population growth, rather than abandon its intransigent dogma.

Fortunately, the refusal to deal realistically with social problems no longer applies to many within the churches, for they have seen that they cannot forever resist social change. Many religious groups have allied themselves with the cause of social reconstruction, even of democracy. This is part of the contemporary effort to humanize religion: The movement for "Christianity with a human face" is an effort to apply the "word of God" to the life of man. The Gospel must be social for the religious liberal, or it is nothing. Granted. But the quest for emancipation of the mind of man, the working out of a new sexual ethic appropriate to new concepts of human nature, and the concern with moral and social reconstruction—all are the product of the immense revolution in scientific knowledge and technology, still impeded by forms of religiosity, still seeking to limit free expression. Can humankind express itself fully while it is still in bondage to vestiges of a primitive theism?

THE PURPOSE OF LIFE

A common religious tradition often enables people to share adversity together. Religious encounters in worship and ceremony tend to lessen tension and anxiety and to give the individual some sense of identification with a larger reality. They are rudimentary explorations in group dynamics and psycho-sociological therapy. Latter-day creeds and codes attempt to do the same thing, by *binding* an individual to a way of life in order to solve his problems and assuage his fears. Religious belief in this sense is evocative and purgative. It attempts to achieve a level of homeostatic equilibrium. Religion has no doubt served its primary function. Out of sorrow and pain it has provided hope, helped to comfort the sick and soothe the forlorn. It is a balm to enable human beings to endure. Its mythology was sheer poetry evocative of the human psyche. Its morality, based in part upon the experience of the race, and love, and brotherhood, was couched in phobia and taboo. It sought to save men by deceiving them, by proffering the myth of God and immortality as a source of moral hope. In order to calm the wavering spirit, it concealed the real nature of the human condition. It prevented men from facing the world authentically. It cultivated instead obedience and submission. It did not permit the development of natural courage. It encouraged cowardice and dependence. Instead of resoluteness and boldness, bravery and confidence in men's powers, it extolled masochism. Acquiescence and awe before the grandeur of the universe were the great virtues, pride the great sin. Theistic religion, particularly in its Judaic-Christian form, thus apotheosized the human failure of nerve.

The basic indictment against the historic role of religion is that it has often sought to thwart man's natural tendency toward audacity, the heroic feat, the great enterprise and achievement of which human beings are capable. The species has both a passive and dominant component; humans are capable of dependence and independence, cowardice and courage, fear and bravery.

Only in the modern world has man been able to assert himself, to develop a new sense of his powers, made possible in large part by the gradual demythologizing of his past and the extension of reason to the control of his problems—a supersession of humanism over antihumanism. The development of courage is enormously enhanced by scientific knowledge and control over nature. In one sense the hope of mankind lies in the furtherance of critical scientific intelligence; in testing claims to truth by logical consistency and experimental confirmation. The overriding need is not to retreat into a new irrationalism, but to apply the methods of critical intelligence to grave social problems. Man cannot live without religion in this sense: he needs to invest his frail life with meaning and purpose. The real question is not *whether* to be religious, but to what kind of religious commitment he can meaningfully devote himself. That theism has failed should be clear to every man. What is still unclear is what will take its place.

II / Marxism as a Religion

The problem for post-modern man is not simply to transcend his past fixation on God, but to create a new and authentic purpose for his existence. But in merely divesting himself of one illusion, there is no guarantee that he will not take on another, and that new forms of antihumanism will not succeed in dehumanizing him. History has shown that as man is ready to seize the initiative and assert himself, he often loses his nerve and retreats in fear. The Hellenistic humanism of Greece and Rome was followed by Christianity and the Dark Ages, the humanism of the Renaissance by the fundamentalism of the Reformation. Today we face a similar situation. Newer forms of antihumanism have appeared. For example, some forms of Marxism are a perversion of an originally humanistic philosophy; millennial creeds of egalitarianism often substitute passionate rhetoric for realistic ameliorative methods; and repressions result from the misuse of

28

scientific technology by a military-industrial-bureaucratized society enamored of its symbols of power and self-righteousness. Powerful antihumanistic tendencies again threaten to deny man the ability to express fully his humanity.

It is not possible to defeat theism by proclaiming a militant atheism. Atheism by itself is simply abstract and meaningless unless it is accompanied by positive recommendations to replace the moral code of theism and resolve man's alienation. A crucial problem of postmodern life is that man is being dehumanized by class or bureaucracy. Using new methods of social organization and technology, he has often become enslaved by the very techniques he has introduced to free himself. The irony of our time is that mankind is threatened by new forms of atheistic ideology which, offering to save him, end up—as with theism—by debasing and exploiting him.

It is important to clarify the sense in which a movement can be said to be religious. The term "religious" may be used to point to a belief in God as the "divine and hidden source of being." If we were to accept this definition in the strict sense, it would apply only to *theistic* beliefs, excluding a whole series of institutional beliefs, attitudes, and practices that are nontheistic, yet have religious characteristics and functions. There are, however, many religions that are nontheistic; hence, a definition should not be so narrow as to exclude them: Buddhism, Confucianism, Epicureanism, Stoicism, for example; theism in any strict interpretation does not easily apply to them. In short, in defining a belief, we should refer to its experiential or behavioral components. *All* religious systems, in my view, are expressions of human behavior, and it is the kind of experience and the way of life they express that is important.

A *religious* experience or way of life involves at least these components:

(a) It offers a solution to the problem of the *meaning* of human life.

(b) It requires *commitment*. This means that there is some moral dedication or devotion, some binding character in a set of ideal beliefs that stimulate motivation and action.

(c) A religious commitment, as distinct from other kinds, is a *basic* or *fundamental* commitment to those ideals that function as first principles.

(d)   Moreover, it differs from mere commitment to a philosophical outlook, which is rationally grounded, or from a commitment to basic postulates or axioms that guide scientific inquiry, because it is at base *infused or charged with emotion and passion.* It appeals to the whole person, going beyond thought and involving feeling and action.
(e)   To be religious also implies an element of *faith,* an affirmation that results in one's staking his life on a certain style or course of action. Most religionists and theologians recognize the role of faith in religious belief.

To avoid confusion over this last element, we must make an important distinction between at least two meanings of the word "faith." First, faith may be a belief that something is true of the world, that is to say, "real," even though it has not been tested or proved. Thus the belief in God as an ultimate reality is a belief in an alleged propositional truth: The believer has faith that God, or X, or some other entity, really exists, though this cannot be fully demonstrated. Because of this leap beyond the evidence, this type of faith is only a reinforcement of a psychological belief-state. When someone asks a believer "Why do you believe in God, or in X?" he may reply, "Because I have faith," that is, he believes because he believes. There are several nontheistic, as well as all theistic, religions that contain this kind of propositional assertion; for example, certain types of belief in the Dialectic or in evolutionary Progress are of this sort, functioning similarly to the God-belief.

On the other hand, there is a second sense of faith which is not propositional, but prescriptive and directive. One may say, "I believe in world government," or "democracy," knowing full well that they do not exist in any perfect form. What one affirms by saying that he believes in them is that he hopes that they will come into being or prevail. Here there is faith in an *ideal* rather than an idea. This kind of faith is *normative.* Some object to the use of the term "religion" in the way that I have used it to refer to basic commitments. I will not quibble and would be willing to use the term "philosophy" or "morality" in place of religion: the main point is the need of the whole person to find direction and focus. Whether a person's religion or philosophy or morality provides that is not crucial.

Now, as I shall argue, some forms of Marxism try to give focus to life, and in doing so they fulfill all the criteria of religion. They offer

(a) meaning and purpose to human existence, and they involve (b) commitment to certain (c) basic principles and ideals that (d) go beyond reason, express passion, and (e) involve a degree of faith, not simply in an idea but in an ideal. Marxism evokes commitment to a hope of a better tomorrow, not through an immortal soul but a just society.

But more, much like some powerful, moving, even fanatic religion, Marxism in some of its manifestations has seized and captured the imagination and dedication of its devotees. This is the primary secret of its appeal: not doctrine, but a passionate commitment to faith. I am not saying that religious faith is bad; given the human condition, some religious commitment—moral and affirmative in character—may indeed be necessary. There are, however, good and bad, constructive and destructive religions. Some create a more serious problem than others in their excessive leap of faith beyond the evidence. Some are based in fantasy and mythology to such a great degree that they distort most of the positive elements of life.

IDEOLOGICAL TRANSFORMATION

Historical trends are difficult to predict. Who, living in classical Rome, could have imagined that Roman civilization would be engulfed by an Asian mystery cult founded by an alleged itinerant and uneducated Jewish carpenter named Jesus? Similarly, who could have believed a century ago that half the world would be overtaken by a religious tidal wave inspired by a poor scholar named Karl Marx, who spent much of his adult life in the British Museum? Yet Marxism has indeed swept half the world and in the other half it is a great attraction for large numbers of alienated intellectuals and young people. Thus a religionized Marxism now competes with a Christianized Judaism for the soul of man. Antihumanistic tendencies have emerged out of the womb of humanistic assumptions.

How explain this perplexing phenomenon? Jesus was hardly correct when he claimed that the Kingdom of God was imminent; nor were his disciples when they proclaimed him the Christ, Son of God. The advent of Christianity was not the fulfillment of God's Word upon Earth. It was, however, a self-fulfilling prophecy; for Jesus prophesied a new birth of faith on earth, and his wish became father to that fact for countless millions of men and generations upon generations of Western civilization. The growth of Christianity no more vindicates the truth of its message than did the latterday growth of Islam verify Mohammedanism. Historically, both religions satisfied deep-felt needs within the human psyche and, once institutionalized, achieved a power and effect far greater than their original impulses. Ideas by themselves are not causative until they are implemented in action; but once they are codified and regulated they take on a life of their own and have effects far greater than originally intended.

Is the growth and power of Marxism to be explained in Marxist terms—that Marx discovered the laws of history in the dialectical process, that he accurately foresaw the development of contradictions between the forces and relationships of production and the eventual replacement of one set of social relations by another? Marx predicted the emergence of proletariat consciousness ready to wrest control from the dominant capitalist class. Is the growth of Marxist consciousness the confirmation of his theory? Or, on the contrary, was Marxist ideology itself the basis for a self-fulfilling prophecy? And is its power to be explained in part by the fact that Lenin, like Paul, discovered that merely to promulgate an idea is not enough, that one needs to reinforce it by a legion of disciplined church or party cadres, who are dedicated to its truth and unquestionably committed to materializing it and defending it against all counter efforts?

There is no doubt that Marx, like Jesus, was a heroic genius, a man possessed of brilliant insight and capable of profundity; and his works attest to the substantial contribution that he has made to philosophy, sociology, and economics. But the power of Marxism cannot be explained solely by his theories; for these were at least partially limited by his 19th-century experience, and they have been superseded by the considerable development of the social sciences. The power of Marxism must therefore be located in its religious impulse and its moral protest.

The theories of Marxism have at least a double function. On the one hand, Marx provided an analysis of society and an explanation of historical change. According to Engels, Marx's writings were unique because of "two great discoveries, the materialistic conception of history and the revelation of the secret of capitalistic production through surplus value."[1] The Marxist theory may thus be considered a scientific-philosophical account of the basic causes of historical change and of the role that certain determining structural factors exert in society—and in recent epochs in capitalist society. Marx's speculations are insightful and provocative and provide a powerful tool for the sociological interpretation of history and society. But they are not omnicompetent to deal with all social changes; they must be modified and supplemented by non-Marxist categories and concepts if we are to understand and explain the dynamics of contemporary life. In any case, Marx, like Aristotle, Machiavelli, Hobbes, Hegel, Freud, and Dewey, has made profound contributions to our understanding of man and society, and these remain as part of our intellectual resources. Even if Marx were the Newton of social science, however—and this is questionable—that would still not explain his tremendous appeal.

I submit that the explanation of this popularity lies in part in another function of Marxist language and philosophy: its moral and religious appeal. For Marx, like Jesus, provides a response to man's existential situation. He offers a set of normative ideals and prescriptions for how we shall live and in what direction we should work; and his message has been transformed by his disciples into a new faith, a new hope, a new promise. As mankind discards one religion, long since debunked and intellectually untenable, it seems all too prone to cleave to another, more sophisticated and subtle, yet clothed with a religious mantle. That Marx has had to suffer the excesses of his misinterpreters is most unfortunate. On which side of the barricades would he have been in a contest with Stalin or Mao? It is not difficult to say; surely, he would be in opposition to the antihumanism of many of his devotees.

I do not mean by these observations to minimize Marx's extremely valuable perceptions of man and society, to deride his moral insights, or to deny the need for drastic social change in the world. Indeed, Marx stands as one of the great humanist moralists; he recognizes the imperative necessity for social reconstruction. It is not Marx but the perversion of Marx that is the seedbed for a new religiosity.

[1] See Friedrich Engels, *Socialism: Utopian and Scientific*, English translation by Edward Aveling, 1892.

The sons of great men are usually lesser men than their fathers; the disciples of geniuses lesser men than their teachers: Christ should not be blamed for Christianity, nor Marx for Marxism. Most likely both would disclaim paternity.

The appeal of Marx is based on his moral sensitivity to poverty and exploitation, oppression and ignorance, and his vision of a more perfect community of men. As a critic of hypocrisy, he would no doubt be a foe of the crimes committed in his name; he expresses profound outrage at what he considers to be the stupidities and inequities in civilization. Mankind, he believes, has progressed far enough in wisdom and power to correct these deficiencies. This was his essential message.

But there have been other critics of social injustices, others who have dreamed of ideal societies in which life was beneficent, peaceful, creative, and productive. History is full of moral indictments and utopian visions. Wherein did Marx differ? Marxism offered no mere promise of immortal life on earth; it offered a concrete set of proposals in *praxis* to realize the goal. In answer to Fourier, Saint-Simon, and Robert Owen and other early socialists, his was a "scientific" and "realistic" socialism, not merely visionary or utopian.

Yet in saying this, Marxism disposed itself to a religious transformation. Given the insecure and often tragic character of human existence, Marxism offered a new ideal in which the limitations and failures of life, based on a corrupt social system, could be overcome; and it held the promise of a new, transformed life in which felicity, justice, and serenity could prevail. It became a secular religion of hope, aimed at alleviating fear and focusing on a better tomorrow.

This moral-religious sense was grounded in a doctrine of dialectical progress which, like theism, was enshrined in a kind of inevitability. The Marxist prophecy was not mere wishful thinking; it was rooted in the nature of reality—not in static being, but in dynamic flux and process, the essence of history. The true believer in communism would suffer oppression by capitalist society, but he would be vindicated in the end by the victory of his ideal; thus his reward lay in the future. Accordingly, a religious hunger rooted itself in the weakest aspect of Marx, his philosophical-metaphysical dialectic of history, and this was used not simply as an empirical tool of analysis —it was useful as that—but as a dogma and creed. Although Marxism was predicated on atheism and science, and rejected theistic non-sense, it nevertheless became for man a fulfillment of functions similar to those that underlay the discarded symbols of theism. This development in Marxism was especially pronounced in its Leninist-Stalinist version. The ideals of socialism degenerated in the Soviet system into a form of state capitalism, which has led to a new kind of authoritarianism even more terrible than the authoritarian church of theism. It has imposed a rigid orthodoxy on philosophy and science and the arts. It has increasingly raised the spectre of repression. In the name of an earlier call for emancipation and liberation of humanity there has emerged a clever new state religion more regimented than any of its predecessors.

Unfortunately, with the death of Stalin and with all the lessons that should have been learned, Marxism has assumed still another religious form in certain varieties of the New Left. Indeed, the neo-Marxist New Left often bears the symptoms of a religious revival in an even more primitive form than the excesses of the old Left. Their religious romanticism has at times threatened to engulf some societies in a kind of antihumanistic barbarism of virtue. Many of the leading proponents of the New Left (such as Marcuse) attacked humanism as a bourgeois hoax. Some observers even saw in this self-righteous moralism the possibility that another dark age may be descending upon man. Five hundred years of post-Renaissance humanism, warned Jacques Barzun, may be at an end; and it may be that the only hope for learning and the humanities will be to found lay monasteries to ride out the impending death of freedom and creativity.[2]

MARX AS A HUMANIST

There is a great irony in the development of Marxism. As I have already indicated, Marx is one of history's great humanist thinkers. Heir to the humanism of Greece and Rome, the Renaissance and the Enlightenment, he expresses the most eloquent values of the free mind. Indeed, his most lasting contribution may be not so much his

[2] "The Conflict of Action and Liberty: The Humanities in the Melting Pot," *The Humanist*, Vol. XXX, no. 5, Sept./Oct., 1970.

theoretical explanations of society and history—instructive as these may be—but his contributions to moral philosophy.

In what sense, then, is Marx a humanist?

First, he is a humanist because he rejects theistic religion and defends atheism. As a materialist, Marx cannot propose a spiritualized view of nature. Mind or consciousness does not have any independent reality, but is only a reflection of matter or body. This view enables Marx to condemn religion for obstructing human development. "Religion," he maintains, "is the sign of the oppressed creature, the sentiment of a heartless world, and the soul of soulless conditions"; or, in his famous phrase, it is "the opium of the people." The abolition of religion and its promise of an illusory happiness is a necessary condition of the demand for "real happiness."[3]

Marx thus shares with other humanist thinkers a distaste for supernaturalism and defends a naturalistic world view. But philosophical or abstract atheism is incomplete, he admonishes in his remarkable *Economic and Philosophic Manuscripts.* Communism begins with atheism; but atheism itself is abstract; "communism is at once *real* and directed on *action.*"[4] "Communism, as fully developed naturalism, equals humanism, and as fully developed humanism equals naturalism." It is, says Marx, "the *genuine* resolution of the conflict between man and nature and between man and man." It is "the riddle of history solved."[5] One cannot simply negate God, as the atheist avers; one must then postulate the existence of man. Communism is the next step, "hence the *actual* phase necessary for the next stage of historical development in the process of human emancipation and rehabilitation."[6]

Marx's view that merely rejecting God is hardly sufficient is indisputable: One must take still other steps forward. Although he thought the next step was his own theory of communism, we may question also whether this is sufficient. Even to move in that direction leaves unsettled many problems of life. The core of his humanism can best be seen in his discussion of the relations between his

[3] Raya Dunaskaya, "Marxism and Humanism" in *The Humanist Alternative,* ed. by Paul Kurtz, London, Pemberton Publishing Co., 1973.
[4] Ed. by Dirk J. Struik, N. Y., International Publishers, 1964, p. 136.
[5] *Ibid.,* p. 135.
[6] *Ibid.,* p. 146.

proposed communism and humanistic values. It is clear that Marx was not interested in communism, that is, the abolition of private property and the destruction of capitalism, for its own sake; but rather for what it achieved. Communism as such is not the end of human development: Man is. Marx wanted man to be free, spontaneous, creative, to realize his potentialities. Instead, he found him repressed, thwarted, deflected from satisfying his real needs and capacities. This deadening of human freedom occurred because of the existence of economic classes; destroy and transform them by means of communism and man might at last be emancipated. Freedom and autonomy are the ultimate ends, but they cannot be achieved within the structure of society as we know it. Marx insists in the *Communist Manifesto* that "the freedom of the individual is the basis of the freedom of all." And in *Das Kapital* that "the development of human power, which is its own end" is the genuine "realm of freedom."[7] *The Grundrisse* (1857) also shows the underlying continuity of Marx's thought.[8] Humanistic concepts are found throughout his work, not merely as a phase of his idealistic youth.

It is the division of labor, according to Marx, that fragments life and compels humans to focus their energies primarily on one form of activity. It is the existence of private property and the fact that their labor is appropriated by someone else that deprives the workers of their humanity. The worker becomes a slave of the objects that he produces. But more, his labor, controlled by others for profit, itself becomes a commodity. "What then constitutes the alienation of labor?" Marx asked.[9] It is the fact that labor is made "external to the worker, that is, it does not belong to his essential being." In his labor, man the worker "does not affirm himself but denies himself," does not feel content, does not freely develop his energy, but mortifies his body and mind. The worker thus "feels outside his work, and in his work feels outside himself." His labor is coerced, not voluntary. It does not satisfy a basic need, but is merely a means to satisfy needs external to it. The worker is thus estranged from both the product of his labor and the act of production. Since he depends upon nature

[7] *Das Kapital*, Kerr edition, Vol. III., pp. 944-54.
[8] Karl Marx, *The Grundrisse*, ed. and translated by David McLellan, N. Y., Harper & Row, Publishers, 1971.
[9] *Economic and Philosophic Manuscripts, op. cit.*, p. 110.

for his life, he is also estranged from nature and from his species' life; his nature as a human being becomes alien to him. As a consequence he is estranged from others, who stand to him in a special kind of relationship. The worker is under the yoke of another who, because of the existence of private property, can control him and consider him as a commodity. The only thing a serf or proletarian has to sell is his labor power, and the lord or capitalist purchases it at a low price, debases human values, and forces the worker into a state of subsistence in which his deepest qualities cannot be fulfilled. Money and exchange value comprise the final debasement. Man must sell himself for a minimal wage, barely enough to keep his family alive.

The indictment continues: Because of profit, rent, and interest, the owner extracts the real source of value, the labor expended, from the worker and retains it for his own use, as in the case of capitalism, for capitalist accumulation. The surplus theory of value on one hand is a description of capital formation in capitalist economies and on the other involves a moral indictment. "Real value" is created by labor, thought Marx, but under an unjust system of social relations it is never fully returned to those who have created it. Marx shows a deep sympathy for the plight of the workingman. Marxist humanism not only exalts freedom but equality and fraternity as ends to be achieved in a just society. The humanist cannot help but be impressed by the moving character of Marx's analysis and of his deep moral vision.

This is no place to enter into a critical analysis of the labor theory or surplus theory of value under capitalism. The question I wish to raise here is whether *all* human alienation may be traced to estranged labor. Surely, modern man is estranged and his labor is fragmented, depersonalized, often devoid of significance; he functions as part of the machine factory and organization system. Moreover, income is disproportionately and unjustly distributed in many societies in which capitalist production prevails.

But even if we were to solve the problem of estranged labor, and redress unfair wage rates, other forms of alienation might ensue. Alienation is pluralistic and cannot be given a simplified explanation; there are various kinds of alienation, based on ethnic, religious, and cultural differences; racism; biological, psychological, and personality traits; the relation of man to nature; and so on. Not all of these may be attributed to the alienation of labor.

Can socialism or communism alone solve even the problem of alienated labor? It has not been solved in socialist or quasi-socialist economies; a new bureaucracy and new class have emerged and the worker is again estranged from his work in large industrial organizations. If Marxism is offered as a solution to the problem of alienated labor and cannot solve it, then Marx's recommendations for social and economic reconstruction may be thrown into question.

Leaving these considerations aside for the moment, however, we must look at Marx's general theory of human nature, including his observations on labor. According to Marx, man is first a producer, and it is the social conditions under which he labors and produces that define his being. "For the socialist man, the *entire so-called history of the world,*" says Marx, "is nothing but the creation of man through human labor."[10] Accordingly, if we can remedy that condition, we can resolve the main problem of social existence. Communism is the means by which alienation is to be solved and human nature fulfilled; the materialistic condition of a society determines its philosophical, ideological, scientific, aesthetic, moral, and religious expressions—elements which reflect the underlying conditions governing the mode of production. Expand the forces of production and reconstruct the relationships of production and you can engender a creative burst of man's aesthetic, moral, and intellectual talents. It is precisely this materialistic interpretation of history—which Engels thought was Marx's major contribution—that is in question. Are the forces and relationships of production, "in the last analysis," "ultimate" and "decisive" in determining human history, as Engels thought? Or can other elements in the superstructure determine the mode of production? There is a direct relationship in history between the technological level of production and the way of life of a people. A slave society is based upon slave power; an agricultural society upon animal power and agricultural techniques; a fishing community of course builds its life about the sea; the steam engine, fossil fuels, and atomic energy have led to dramatic leaps in technology and in the way communities live and work.

[10] *Economic and Philosophic Manuscripts, op. cit.,* p. 145.

The great recent changes in society can be traced to technological advances related to scientific discovery and invention—intellectual and ideological elements that intervene in the forces of production. "Consciousness" may have a more significant role than elements in the so-called material base. Consciousness is not merely a reflection of this base. The productive ability of a people does not depend simply upon the relationships of production and whether or not they are fetters on the forces of production; rather it depends upon a constellation of values, moral and philosophical concepts. History cannot be understood as a product of one factor, as Engels recognized, because other factors intervene and modify the social structure. Although the economic interpretation of history may be, within limits, a useful analytic guide, it is not a total theory of society; nor does it serve, by itself, as a sufficient ground for normative morality or social policy.

What is seminal in Marx's humanism is that, unlike previous humanisms, it does not hold that one can save man from alienation merely by reforming him or making him rational, or by espousing ideals of justice and virtue. Emancipation is a *social* problem. It is only by a radical change in the social system, not by a conversion of the individual, that the human condition can be ameliorated. One cannot have a just man in an unjust society. It is *every* man, in social terms, not each man, that must be the starting point. For Marx, man is a social animal, the essence of him is tied up with his social relations. Given this conception, the problem of alienation can only have a social solution; it is the *structure* that must be changed, and the relationships that men bear to one another; the existing social classes must be destroyed if mankind is to recover its humanity.

In this basic Marxian insight there is both power and limitation. While one must agree that many, indeed most, human problems have a social solution, one need not say that *all* do. There are individual biologically and psychologically based determinants of human behavior. Although a change in the structure of society is essential, whether it is sufficient is questionable. A new social system may bring in its wake even more terrible forms of oppression. There are questions for which we today have no easy solution, particularly in the light of the Marxists' efforts to remake economic and social structures. That they have succeeded dramatically in ameliorating the life of the average working man or improving his economic and cultural standard of living, in comparison with other economic systems in the world, is doubtful. Mere seizure of the instruments of production is no panacea. To transfer power without humanizing it makes little advance in the human condition.

An essential indication of Marx's humanism is the central role which he entrusts to reason. This faith in reason is continuous with the humanism of classical Greece. For Marx, the history of mankind has heretofore been governed by blind and uncontrolled forces, of which the participants have been unaware. Moral reconstruction can occur only with social reconstruction; and this can only be achieved by a rational understanding of the causes of our alienation and a reordering of society in terms of them. In short, Marx, insofar as he expresses a profound trust in reason and science, as he understood them, is a direct heir of the Enlightenment.

He uses reason to attack illusion, not only the mythology of religious illusion, but the pomposity and narrowness of moral shibboleths. He shows that religions and moral ideals often mask underlying economic and class interests. Values are relative. To glorify them as abstract and eternal is to miss their historical role in a social system and their consequent limitations. As Marx wished to develop the social sciences, he relied heavily on scientific modes of explanation. It is true that his science is limited by its Hegelian rationalistic and metaphysical components. Nevertheless, it was "scientific socialism" that Marx talked about, based, in principle at least, upon the use of the scientific method. He envisioned the use of applied reason, functioning as an "art" or as "practical wisdom" in classical terms or as a "policy science" in recent terms. The crucial point is that Marx thought the solution to human estrangement could come about in part by a self-conscious awareness of its existence and in part by a determination to use intelligence in order to redirect social forces into new and meaningful channels. He had confidence in man's ability to order and plan his destiny and to rebuild it by use of the natural principles discovered by science. Although man is a laboring animal, he is also capable of reason; and reason becomes the instrument, once embodied in *praxis,* of social transformation. Marx condemns the mere abstract contemplative use of reason; he lauds its concrete applications.

Marxism, then, is an expression of humanistic courage. Unlike theism, it does not have a low estimate of the capacities of man. On the contrary, Marx had no illusion about reality. For man, life itself is the chief good, and it can be lived badly or well. All men seek a significant and enriched existence. If they cannot achieve the good life, it is because they are dominated by irrational and unjust social forces. Release them from these forces and provide positive conditions for the satisfaction of their needs, and the opportunity for development and the good life in a just society can be achieved. Marx had little doubt about the perfectibility of man; he thought his imperfections could be remedied, his tribulations alleviated, his anxieties quieted; if only man would face his condition and turn his efforts toward justice. Thus Marxist-humanism is life-affirming and optimistic; it has confidence in positive human powers; and it believes that, given proper conditions, they will eventually prevail.

THE RELIGIOUS PERVERSIONS OF MARXISM

The betrayal by latter-day Marxists of Marxism's essential morality and the undermining of its ameliorative view of man is especially distressing to serious students of Marx. What we are confronted with is the existence of antihumanistic elements side by side with humanism. These tendencies existed implicitly not only in Marx's theories but in his complex personality.

Lewis Feuer in *Marx and the Intellectuals*[11] draws a highly uncomplimentary portrait of Marx the man. According to Feuer, at the same time that Marx was willing to sacrifice himself for humanity, he had an utter contempt for human beings. "Moreover, he seemed to exalt struggle and conflict." Surely, we should not commit the genetic fallacy and condemn a theory because of the personality of its formulator. In Marx's writings we do find a strange mixture of humanism and antihumanism. Did Marx fully appreciate the subtleties of the human person, and does Marxism as a theory give sufficient weight to these components? Or was Marx so committed to his brilliant insight into the nature of man—the economic determinants overlooked by others—that he excluded other aspects of life? In particular, a

[11] N. Y., Doubleday, 1969.

central conflict emerges in his writings: an intolerance of intolerance, a hatred of injustice, an impatience with the errors and foibles of ordinary human beings.

The strange relationship between means and ends is the fundamental paradox that besets Marx and the Marxists. In Marx's view utopian socialists failed to create a just society because they did not attend to the practical kinds of action. But can we use any means to achieve humanistic ends? What about the tendency to hatred and intolerance? What of the use of violence and revolution? If Marx was a humanist in ideal ends, he was not a humanist in his moral principles. Engels made clear his belief in the extreme relativism of all moral considerations when he said:

> We . . . reject every attempt to impose on us any moral dogma whatsoever as an eternal, ultimate, and forever immutable moral law on the pretext that the moral world too has its permanent principles which transcend history and the differences between nations. We maintain on the contrary that all former moral theories are the product, in the last analysis, of the economic stage which society has reached at that particular epoch. And as society has hitherto moved in class antagonisms, morality was always a class morality . . . A really human morality which transcends class antagonisms and their legacies in thought becomes possible only at a stage of society which has not only overcome class contradictions but has even forgotten them in practical life. . .[12]

On the contrary, one may argue, without adhering to a doctrine of an absolute moral law, that there should be an independent role for an ethical humanism of principles; and certain principles can transcend the material base of a society. Truth, honesty, sympathy, kindness are humanistic virtues that are not time-bound even though they must be given a contextual interpretation. In any social system, if men are to live and work together in some sort of cooperative endeavor, then certain ethical principles ought to be respected.

Underlying the Marxist approach, however, is a basic, violent intolerance of alternative ideals and points of view concerning what is "progressive" and what is "reactionary" in social movements. One

[12] Engels in *Anti-Dühring* (1878, pp. 103-7) quoted in Howard Selsam and Harry Martel, *Reader in Marxist Philosophy*, N. Y., International Publishers, 1963, p. 252.

might ask: How can a new world of cooperative relationships be built on the dead corpses of hatred? Tolerance should be a cardinal principle of any moral idealism that claims to be progressive. This does not mean that we should tolerate unjust conditions, nor that we should not seek to radically change attitudes and behavior. Yet the kind of self-righteous moralism that pervades Marxist literature is much like the impatient severity that classical theism—especially during the Inquisition—directed against opposing points of view. One cannot help feeling Marx's overpowering sneer at those with whom he disagrees; rather than maintaining indulgence toward contrary opinions, Marx is angry with the hypocrisies and stupidities of his opponents. Much of his attitude is predicated upon the notion that the major division in society is the conflict of classes; hence, hatred and struggle against the rulers is inevitable. But can a new world be built on bitterness? Marx did not blame the individual member of the bourgeoisie, only the system that made him what he was. But intolerance of a system inevitably spills over to those who occupy its seats of power, and also to those who compromise with it.

Marx's theory of class only exacerbates antagonisms, even where they did not exist before. Democratic anarchism is naive; neither a socialist nor a capitalist society can function without elites. The need is to make certain that membership in an elite is based upon ability. Membership should be open to all, with equality of opportunity for people to rise to the levels of their capability. An elite should not be dominated by self-interest, nor selected by considerations of power or wealth. It must be innovative if it is to contribute to the common good. There is an elite under capitalism, increasingly the corporate managers rather than owners; and there is an elite under state socialism, the bureaucrats who are members of the Party. Marx's hatred for the elite, which he defends under the guise of class warfare, may do more to limit progress than to enhance it. The problem for workers in all societies is to get elites to be receptive to criticism, to hold them to account, to make them more responsive, to humanize their use of power.

The overriding problem that has split the world socialist movement concerns the means of bringing socialism about. This problem split the social democrats from the Leninist-Stalinists, the socialist parties from the communist parties, and was at the center of debate within the New Left. Marx recognized that to espouse a moral idealism or utopian vision is not enough, that preachments are no substitute for action. He thought we needed an appraisal of the locus of power and the ways to destroy or reorder it. No class, he said, ever willingly gives up its power. If mankind is to achieve communism, it can only be by means of battle. The Marxist must be a revolutionary. He must be willing to smash the old social system, wrest control from the hands of the masters, and seize the means of production. Violence may be the only means available to force the issue. According to Lewis Feuer, Marx's socialist program is built upon a strategy of aggression and hatred, not love or compromise. "To reject violence," according to Engels, was the "parson's mode of thought—lifeless, insipid, and impotent."[13] In defending the use of hatred in Germany, he says: "In our country it is hatred rather than love that is needed —at least in the immediate future—and more than anything else a shedding of the last remnants of German idealism."[14]

It is true that there are portions of Marx and Engels that admit the use of peaceful democratic means to achieve socialism. Yet this is only one aspect of a revolutionary ideology that extolled the use of violence, emphasized struggle, and ruled out limitation by ethical principles as a kind of "modern mythology." All of this has been the seedbed for Stalinist perversions of Marxism, which continues to be weighed with an ambivalent and contradictory moral position: It rejects modern society because of the hatred and injustice, cruelty and oppression in it; it focuses on an ideal state of moral perfection; nevertheless, it is itself ready to use hatred and violence to achieve the good as it conceives it. How ideal ends can be reconciled with a morality of evil means is the unresolved dilemma of Marxism.

The retort usually made to these doubts is that unless there is an uncompromising struggle against capitalism, socialism will not come into being. To which one must in turn retort: But at what price? Is

---

[13] Friedrich Engels, *Herr Eugen Dühring's Revolution in Science,* trans. Emil Burns, N. Y., International Publishers, pp. 209-10.
[14] From Karl Marx and Friedrich Engels, *Selected Correspondence,* Moscow ed., 1953, pp. 367-68.

the struggle worthwhile if in the process of achieving one's ends one betrays and brutalizes them by terrible means? To answer affirmatively is to invoke antihumanism, defended as revolutionary in the name of humanism: an antihumanistic humanism.

One of the sources of this intolerance may be traced to a first metaphysical principle of Marxism, and the degree of conviction with which it is held. I am referring here to the dialectical materialism to which both Marx and Engels were committed. If one is convinced that there are laws in history and that one has discovered them, then those in opposition to the thrust of history are seen as morally wrong; one's cause is morally right and just.

But what can be said of this dialectic, which is perhaps the most important yet the weakest axiom of the Marxist *Weltanschauung?* Positivists and empiricists have attacked it on at least two grounds: first, because it is an unverified thesis, and second and more devastatingly, because it is nonfalsifiable. The highly general assumption that history moves by dialectical laws—thesis, antithesis, and synthesis, and the contradiction between opposing forces—has not been confirmed by the social sciences or historical inquiry. The dialectical laws of Hegel may be questioned on epistemological grounds, as too formal and abstract to allow for concrete interpretation; and the more specific economic or sociological interpretation of history, that is, Marx's special application of the dialectic to human affairs, though immensely creative, is also so general that it has not been adequately tested; moreover there appear to be many exceptions to the operation of the "laws." The dialectic lacks sufficient empirical meaning; yet it is offered to explain facts of social and historical existence.

According to Engels:

> The materialist conception of history starts from the proposition that the production of the means to support life—and, next to production, the exchange of things produced—is the basis of all social structure; that in *every* society that has appeared in history, the manner in which wealth is distributed and society divided into classes or orders is dependent upon what is produced, how it is produced, and how the products are exchanged. From this point of view the final causes of all social changes and political revolutions are to be sought not in men's brains, not in man's better insight into eternal truth and justice,

but in changes in the modes of production and exchange.[15] (italics added)

The theory promises too much; it is all-encompassing in its effort to reduce the diversity of social phenomena to a basic set of final and ultimate causes that are supposed to apply to *every* society, however important the economic factors may be in social systems undergoing change. Marx's theory in the last analysis is a quasi-philosophical-poetic theory more than a scientific hypothesis. It resists confirmation and is accordingly, as Karl Popper pointed out, not only unconfirmed but nonfalsifiable. How would we go about testing its assertions? Perhaps by reference to specific cases, by example and illustration of the theory. There are some striking examples, but these surely cannot confirm a total theory. Perhaps what is meant is that theory is tested by *verstehen,* by an intuitive method of apprehension. This is appealed to by some; but not everyone has the same *verstehen* or intuition. Some say that Marx's theory can be tested by experience and by its concrete predictions, but there are serious difficulties here. There is an intimate connection in human affairs between ideas and the events they are supposed to explain; often the ideas are self-creative, mobilizing the very forces needed to confirm them. In short, the truth of the sociological interpretation of history in part is created by espousal of the theory. The ideas, rather than explaining human action, create and mold it. Thus Marxism in part is true because men having studied Marxism, believe in it, and behave accordingly.

The Marxist theory, then, like many others in history, is originative of the very factors that it claims operate in history. This is especially the case when a theory offered as an explanation is actually a prescription. The sociological theory of history and the language in which it is stated is first and foremost normative, directive, expressive. A religious component intervenes in a theory when men no longer consider it dispassionately—to be weighed and tested like all other critical scientific hypotheses—but emotively, requiring above all allegiance. If this is the case, then the theory is nonfalsifiable as a descriptive scientific explanation, since it functions primarily im-

[15] Friedrich Engels, *Socialism: Utopian and Scientific,* translated by Edward Aveling, N. Y., International Publishers, 1935.

peratively and persuasively. Marxism is, if it is anything, a moral and religious declaration of intent and promise.

But there are a great number of predicted events that did not occur as expected in the century after Marx's death. Socialism did not occur by a revolution of the proletariat in advanced industrial societies, but rather in backward, semi-feudal, and underdeveloped societies such as Russia, China, and Cuba. The proletariat in the advanced industrial countries did not develop full class consciousness, as expected, but were often the most "reactionary" elements of the society. In the affluent capitalist societies, the worker was not reduced to a subsistence level; instead his condition improved immeasurably. Capitalist countries did not limit production by monopoly restrictions, but expanded markets by increasing wages and reducing prices; they did not bog down in economic collapse, but were often restored by compensatory fiscal policies adopted by governments accepting Keynesian recommendations. Socialization of the means of production did not lead to a reduction of alienation or a marked improvement in the standard of living or freedom for the workers beyond what was accomplished in capitalist countries, nor did it destroy the class system, but only replaced an old bureaucratic class with a new one. These are only some of the empirical factors that confront Marxist theorists.

In retort, many Marxist scholars talk about capitalism's *impending* collapse in a gigantic economic crash, or of the lowering of the standard of living of the workers, or of the future growth of proletarian consciousness. Some of this may eventuate—history is more often contingent than determinate or fixed—indeed, the Marxist may help to bring it about by a self-fulfilling prophecy. But verification is always in the future, hence the theory is nonfalsifiable and is modified *ad hoc* so as to account for discrepancies by rationalization. The test for a Marxist, more often than not, is a coherence test; all parts of his system of concepts and explanations must fit together. But under what conditions, if any, will it ever be said that the theory is false? Apparently none, for the true believer. His theory cannot be verified, even in principle.

In the last analysis the theory functions, like the God idea, as a *Weltanschauung,* giving coherence and unity to a point of view and moral guidance and direction to a way of life. While scientific humanism involves commitment to a critical rational mode of inquiry as tested by experience, Marxism in its first principle—the dialectic—abandons critical, experimental and practical reason and substitutes a vision of moral poetry and mythology for the real world.

THE INDIVIDUAL

Another crucial question that may be asked of any theory that claims to be concerned with man is what happens to the individual. Marx claims to speak for the individual, to rescue him from a repressive social system, so that he may lead a free and creative existence. But the focus of Marx, as of Hegel, is not the individual, but the social structure and historical process. Are there not some problems of life that have only an individual, not a larger social or historical solution? Do not my cares, my values, my tastes and talents have some primacy? What guarantee do we have that the individual will not be smothered by the social relations that, according to Marx, define him? I am posing here a primarily moral question, concerning the ends of Marxism, not simply its means. It involves a somewhat different conception of human nature than Marx's. We must ask whether Marx fully appreciates the uniqueness of individuality, as Mill does, for example, in *On Liberty*. Does he really believe in the free creative personality who pursues his own life style, who satisfies his own needs and desires as he wishes, who realizes his destiny on his own terms? It must be granted that no man is an island unto himself, that the problems of the individual often have social solutions, that individuality is fully realized only in social contexts. Yet should there not be reserved to individual personalities some measure of privacy? Marx talks about the freedom to fulfill one's nature, but does he appreciate the liberty to be left alone? May I not make my own mistakes and suffer for them, or discover my own truths and live for them? Why should others decide what is good for me; why can't I decide for myself, even if I am in error?

Here liberalism and Marxism diverge. For the humanism of the liberal-humanist, unlike that of the Marxist-humanist, focuses on the individual rather than on the social good. This emphasis on the dignity and value of the individual cannot be dismissed as a mere reflection of bourgeois free enterprise. It transcends each and every social system; indeed, a social system can be evaluated by whether or not it preserves or enhances the rights of free agents.

This difference of ideal ends and values between Marxist-humanism and liberal-humanism must not be underestimated; it has immense practical significance. Liberal humanism cherishes civil liberties, intellectual, aesthetic, moral, and political liberties, dissent and heresy. Marxism at times dismisses them or is willing to compromise them in the revolutionary struggle. The virtues of the commune are overvalued and the virtues of individuality undervalued. The tragedy of modern communist societies is that they have abandoned these fundamental human rights—as the Soviet Union, Hungary, Poland and Czechoslovakia illustrate. Moreover, we may ask whether these rights were ever central in communist theory. Marx said he believed in them and defended the extension of democracy as a progressive program. Within Marxist literature, however, there are priorities and the liberty of individualism is not as high on the scale as are social justice, equality, and fraternity. But can there ever be a just or humane society in which individual liberty is not respected as a *first principle?* Is not socialism *without* democracy as a necessary and uncompromisable principle a contradiction? Can the individual be sacrificed to "progress," the revolution, the party, or mankind; do these not exist for the individual?

On balance, we may say that Marx is a humanist; his humanism far outweighs any nonhumanistic features of his system. Insofar as we have accentuated certain antilibertarian and antihumanistic aspects, it is because of what has happened to his ideas. Perhaps it is the fate of all moral visionaries to be betrayed by their disciples. In what follows I wish to discuss how the scales have toppled the other way and how Marx was confounded by his interpreters. His ideas have become official doctrine, sanctified by the Party-Church, proclaimed and enforced by a priesthood, taken as gospel orthodoxy. The cruel hoax of history is that the great heretic has been invoked to suppress heresy, the dissenter to crush dissenters, the deviationist to crush revisionism. Marxism has become for many an antihumanistic religion.

III / Aftermath of Marx

DISTORTIONS OF MARXIST IDEOLOGY

It is unfortunate that socialism was first tried in Russia, for that vast land had had little, if any, experience with free democratic institutions. The repression of Russian Czardom and nationalism proved to be stronger forces than Marx's humanism; and Marxism has ever since been molded by the straitjacket of that socio-cultural context in which it first came to power. History has repeatedly shown how difficult it is to maintain the initial idealism and enthusiasm of a revolutionary movement; the moral vitality is often followed by atrophy. The conservative reaction after the American Revolution and the continued existence of slavery for ninety years in spite of the Declaration of Independence and the Bill of Rights, and the Napoleonic betrayal of the French Revolution, have striking analogues in the Soviet Union. In such developments, we can discern a disparity between ideals and reality, between the proclamation of a program and its implementation.

The two principal figures in Soviet Marxism who gave it their own indelible stamps were, of course, Lenin and Stalin. Both were professional revolutionaries who from early age were inspired by the vision of a just society. Lenin died a dictator, but began a legend; Stalin died a despot, who had sought to be a god. Both men were responsible for founding a state church, and for institutionalizing Marxism as an official religion.

A religious impulse, whether theistic or nontheistic, grows out of an existential commitment to a way of life, the answer to a quest for meaning and direction, but more often than not it is then institutionalized, becoming part of a new orthodox tradition and law. The religious response, which may be a vital satisfaction of a moral need, becomes wooden and hollow. There are two kinds of religious responses: (1) The original source within the experience of an individual, who has not inherited the religion but has undergone conversion to a new faith within his lifetime and is infused by its moral and emotional appeal. This was true of the early committed Christian and of the revolutionary. (2) The institutionalization of a religion and its transmission to succeeding generations by means of tradition and in a codified form. Individuals who enter church or party accept the doctrine, which may at times move or inspire them; usually they are without fundamentalist fervor. They are nominal believers; not powerless and critical of things as they are, but entrenched in power and part of the establishment. A similar fate, though to a lesser extent, has befallen liberalism in the West, where the faith proclaimed by parents became mere rhetoric of the Establishment for their children.

It was the special organizational skills of Lenin that made the Bolshevik Revolution possible in Russia. He developed a theory of the Communist Party that he was able to put into practice. It was this Party apparatus, first under Lenin, then under Stalin, that solidified Bolshevism's power and transformed it into an institution under the dictatorship of the proletariat, giving Marxism a new direction which has since been called Leninism. According to Stalin, "Leninism is Marxism in the era of imperialism and proletarian revolution. To be more exact, Leninism is the theory and tactics of the proletarian revolution in general and the theory and tactics of the dictator-ship of the proletariat in particular."[1]

The first problem that Lenin faced was to bring the Bolsheviks to power. He thought this could be done only by forging a conspira-torial revolutionary organization. The task was to use every means possible, legal and illegal, to smash the machinery of the bourgeois state. Lenin disagreed with those social democrats, such as Edouard Bernstein and Karl Kautsky, who were willing to use parliamentary and legal methods to bring about socialism peacefully. The long-range strategy of the Party was to destroy the bourgeois system; only the short-range tactics must be adapted to existing conditions. The Party would, for example, participate in the Duma (Russian Parlia-ment) when the tactics of retreat called for this; but eventually more decisive revolutionary action must be used. Lenin was faced with the problem that the masses in Russia had not developed proletarian consciousness, and he could not wait for a democratic majority to de-velop. Hence, he would need to marshal and train a vanguard of highly disciplined and dedicated professional revolutionaries, who would be the advance detachment of the working class, toiling every day to produce revolution.

Lenin's conception of the Party is masterful and bold. It adds a new dimension to Marxist ideology for it involves a supreme test of loyalty. The Party worker is *bound* to the Party, much as the Chris-tian is bound to the church. The Party becomes the official interpre-ter of the Word, defining and applying it to specific conditions. It can brook no compromise or deviation from its line. "Certainly, al-most everyone now realizes," said Lenin, "that the Bolsheviks could not have maintained themselves in power . . . without the strictest, truly iron discipline."[2] "The Communist Party will be able to per-form its duty only if it is organized in the most centralized manner, if iron discipline bordering on military discipline prevails in it, and if its Party center is a powerful and authoritative organ, wielding wide powers and enjoying the universal confidence of the members of the

[1] Joseph Stalin, *The Foundations of Leninism,* Introduction (quoted in Arthur P. Mendel, *Essential Works of Marxism,* N. Y., Bantam, 1961, p. 210).
[2] Vol. XXV, p. 173, as quoted by Stalin in *The Foundations of Leninism, op. cit.,* Mendel, p. 290.

Party."[3] Indeed, Lenin warned, "whoever . . . weakens in the least the iron discipline of the party of the proletariat . . . actually aids the bourgeoisie against the proletariat."[4]

Stalin, as Party secretary, fully approved Lenin's view. Moreover, during the period when the dictatorship of the proletariat was being consolidated, he said that the Party "cannot afford to be 'liberal' or to permit factions." Hence Lenin, he said, demanded "complete elimination of all factionalism," and the "immediate dissolution by expulsion from the Party of all groups, without exception, that have been formed on the basis of various non-Party platforms." Although there can be discussion, disagreement, self-criticism within the Party before a decision is made, once it has been made there can be no dissent. And Stalin adds that "ruthless struggle against these dissenting elements" is a scientific struggle against imperialism. The Party, he said in 1924, must "purge itself of the opportunistic pollutors."

The strict Leninist-Stalinist Communist Parties throughout the world have followed this pattern fairly closely. The Party has operated like an army made up of highly trained cadres, following strict orders. This in my judgment is the "secret weapon" of Marxism: the brilliant insight of Lenin that power in a society, especially during a national crisis, can be seized if there is a tightly-knit army ready and able to move, even if it is only a small minority of the population. Much of this is familiar; yet the remarkable feature of it is the similarity between the dedicated party worker and the priest or nun. The Party becomes the center of moral involvement; it sweeps up and possesses the individual who is nothing separate and distinct from it, and who owes it obedience and devotion. Lenin talks about the organic character of the Party. *"Formerly,"* he said, "our Party was not a formally organized whole. . . . *Now* we have become an organized Party, and this implies the establishment of authority, or the transformation of the power of ideas into the power of authority, the subordination of lower Party bodies to higher Party bodies."[5]

The free mind and free spirit, the individual, his destiny and ideals, are transcended. The religion, at first an existential choice, now be-

[3] Vol. XXV, pp. 282-83, *op. cit.*, p. 291.
[4] Vol. XXV, p. 190, *ibid.*
[5] Vol. VI, p. 291, *op. cit.*

comes a collective concern, and the true believer is wedded to the Party as he was formerly wedded to the church. Ideology has replaced theology as the bearer of salvation to the faithful—but it requires complete obedience to its will. Therein is the basis for a new ethic of repression of the individual and the justification for a totalitarian society led by a Party of Truth, which hence can do no wrong. If the Party and the revolutionary cause become greater than the individual, then individuals begin to lose their dignity and value and are sacrificed to the new level of "revolutionary morality." Even Leon Trotsky, who was later to be an intractable foe of Stalinism, justified the use of terror. When Karl Kautsky in *Terrorism and Communism* (1919) criticized mass executions, the taking of hostages, and other excesses of the Bolsheviks, Trotsky attacked his "Quaker babble about the sanctity of life" and "Kantian preaching." He insisted that "the revolution demands from the working class to achieve its end by *all* means that are at its disposal. . . . The question of the form or the severity of reprisals is not, of course, a question of 'principle.' It is a question of expedience."[6]

Trotsky's view of moral principles can be traced to both Marx and Engels. But while one may argue about the use of terror to achieve a revolution—although serious questions can be raised about its moral justification—it is another thing to justify its continued use after the revolution has been achieved. Perhaps those accustomed to using violence to achieve a noble end may never learn to abandon its use. This is precisely what happened in the Soviet Union. The communists there faced a twofold problem of transition. First, how to bring about the revolution. They made a choice: by any means, however brutal, including violence and bloodshed. Second, once the means of production were seized, how to create a communist society. Again they made a choice: any means to achieve their ends. Marx's ideal humanism of ends was debased by the abandonment of an ethical humanism of principles. The fanatic, observed Santayana, is one who redoubles his efforts long after he has forgotten his goals. The systematic use of Stalinist terror continued after the revolution and

---

[6] Quoted in S. Stojanovic, "Revolutionary Teleology and Ethics," in *Tolerance and Revolution,* ed. by P. Kurtz and S. Stojanovic, Belgrade, Philosophical Society of Serbia, 1970, pp. 46-47.

continues, though to a far lesser degree, today. Under Stalin the Soviet Union was transformed into a police state. There are causal explanations for this; the need for the Soviet Union to industrialize and collectivize rapidly forced Stalin to extract capital from the masses, and this meant the most stringent methods. The tragedy is that it continued to be justified on *moral* grounds. Although the Soviet Union was able to industrialize rapidly, it did so at great cost (Japan and other countries have industrialized, perhaps more rapidly than the Soviet Union, yet without such toll in human misery.)

The bloody story of Stalin's reign and his systematic use of terror is universally known. Stalin emerged as the strongest individual within the Party by destroying his opposition (Zinoviev, Kamenev, Bukharin, Rykov, Trotsky, and so on); he engaged in wholesale purges of communists, constructed an extensive secret police apparatus, allowed the kulaks to starve in order to collectivize the farms, set up an extensive network of labor camps in which millions were imprisoned and died. He shattered all the dreams of idealistic Bolsheviks. The dictatorship not only crushed bodies, but sought to control minds. In the name of Marxism—heir of the great heritage of free thought—Stalin destroyed Marxism and free thought. Censorship and suppression, which the great revolutionary socialists of the world had opposed so bitterly under bourgeois society, was forcefully imposed by an all-powerful totalitarian state, which had not "withered away" and showed no signs of doing so. The infallible Party laid down orthodoxy in all spheres of thought and life. All forms of Party democracy gave way to "democratic centralism," which is another term for obedience to the dictates of those in power.

Leszek Kolakowski, the Polish philosopher, who was expelled from the Communist Party and forced to leave Poland, describes how Stalinism divided the world into orthodoxy and heresy and how all who criticized or disagreed with its policy were condemned. A new class thus emerged, which attempted to sanctify its rule; and even though Stalinism is dead, a new form of neo-Stalinism remains to justify its rule:

> Stalinism's permanent method aimed essentially at creating a situation in which every criticism of Stalinism objectively constituted automatic relegation to the camp of reaction, an automatic declaration of solidarity with capitalism imperialism. Stalinism frustrated any social

criticism and constantly tried to attribute it to counter-revolutionary attitudes.

For centuries death by fire was reserved for heretics rather than pagans and the proscribed books on the Catholic Church's *Index* are rarely those of non-Catholics. That special merciless hatred which almost every organization with a political ideology bestows on its heretics, dissidents, apostles or renegades, a hatred surpassing a hundredfold the most violent revulsion felt toward the recognized enemy, is in reality an understandable product of such social conditions. . . .

Stalinism is a way of life of a political sect. A Stalinist-type party is one which has ceased to treat itself as a means but has become an end in itself. . . .

By surrounding itself with an impenetrable ideological and ritualistic crust, Stalinism . . . not only determines its own course, but all the rest of social reality is also determined by its relationship to Stalinism . . . . The world is divided into the saved and damned, into the City of God and the city of the devil, between which the boundaries are clearer than between a mountain top and a valley. . . . Between the two kingdoms there are neither neutral nor mixed areas: one can only be absorbed by one of them. Because of this, Stalinism demanded either total acceptance or total rejection . . . . Every new ritual and confirmed truth had to be accepted on the threat of complete exclusion from the community of the saved . . . . Stalinism imposed upon the consciousness of the left the fatalism of choosing between heaven and hell, and paralyzed criticism by treating it as the automatic ticket to the camp of reaction.[7]

What is the value of socialist utopia if achieving it entails man's spiritual death and a new kind of suffering? Daniel, Sinyavsky, Galanskov, Ginzburg, Litvinov, Bukovsky, Yesenen-Volpin and Medvedev have been imprisoned in recent years for expressing elementary demands for human rights, as the Soviet writers Isaac Babel and Osip Mandelstam were imprisoned in the early days of Stalinist terror. The more recent heretics, such as the physicist Sakharov and the novelist Solzhenitsyn, have argued for humanistic freedom, much as courageous writers during the Renaissance fought against a repressive church. The free spirit of man that Marx wished to rescue from

[7] Leszek Kolakowski, *The Conspiracy of Ivory Tower Intellectuals.* Quoted from Arthur P. Mendel, *The Essential Works of Marxism, op. cit.,* pp. 357-360.

alienation has become entrapped in a system of methodical repression as terrible as that which existed in the worst days of the Czarist regime.

Undoubtedly the workers and peasants live better now in the Soviet Union than they have at any time before (they do in most of the developing industrial nations). But has the Soviet Union solved the problem of estranged labor? Must man be repressed to be equal? Must the Communist, like Faust, sell his soul to Mephistopheles for utopia?

Many of Eastern Europe's astute critics, such as Djilas, Markovic, Petrovic, and Stojanovic in Yugoslavia, Kolakowski from Poland, and Kosik, Svitak, and Kovaly from Czechoslovakia, are convinced that the problem of alienated labor, the crucial issue for Marx's humanism, which communism was supposed to eliminate, has not been solved. Indeed, the old bourgeois masters have only been replaced by a new class which comprises the Party, the bureaucracy, the technological and managerial elite that run the state. It is a class that enjoys much more power than the capitalists ever enjoyed; it has a total monopoly of both political and economic power; and it permits no major dissent or criticism of its policies and programs. According to Djilas the new class in effect functions as the *owner* of the collective property. Like the corporate managers in capitalist countries, but with far greater power, it administers and controls the state property. This is not the first instance of collective ownership. The Catholic Church, for example, also owns collective property which is administered by the hierarchy. Moreover, as members of an exclusive club or inner circle, they enjoy special privileges, commensurate with their positions of power. Socialist ownership, says Djilas, is a hoax; in actuality it is the bureaucrat who functions as the real owner. Careerism dominates for the functionary. Status and power are his main interest. The luxuries he receives depend on how high he rises in the bureaucracy. The social situation of the communist who has at his disposal an automobile, a good apartment and dacha, regular vacations, and high salary is different, observed Trotsky, from that of the coal miner who received fifty to sixty rubles a month. And there are special privileges for the children of the elite, who inherit them from the power conferred upon their parents. As a consequence, a new form of class inequality and class antagonism emerges. It is the members of the new class who are opposed to freedom and resist any effort to question their power. This appears to confirm Marx's observation that no class will ever willingly relinquish its power.

There were great hopes that with the death of Stalin the system of repressive terror that he created would disappear. The worst aspects of the Soviet system have been eliminated; the police state has become more civilized, less prone to use brutal force. There are those who have read this as preface to a convergence between Western capitalist countries, which would become more socialist-welfare oriented, and the Soviet Union, which would become more democratic. It has been thought that the Soviet system, mellowed with age, would grant concessions to its people and satisfy their hunger for freedom. There were exciting promises, especially during Khruschev's thaw, that this was indeed occurring. With an improvement in the average person's standard of living and with an increase in educational opportunities, and the development of a highly sophisticated managerial-technological class, the demands for freedom would be difficult to resist. This may very well eventuate; it is difficult to accept the idea of a permanent enslavement of men's minds.

Yet the events of the past few years leave little hope for immediate improvement; for Marxist-humanism in Eastern Europe, which reached its highest expression during the Prague spring of 1968, now seems virtually crushed. There were great efforts by Dubcek and others in Czechoslovakia to "create socialism with a human face," to liberalize, to grant civil liberties, intellectual, aesthetic, and cultural freedoms. The Stalinist response proved that nationalism has not disappeared under communism, and indeed—as may be seen in the protests of the Czechs and the Russian reaction—may be a stronger force than socialism. Those events also revealed the fear of the state bureaucracy that it would lose its control if it extended freedom, as well as the fear that similar demands would spread to other countries in Eastern Europe and the Soviet Union itself.

Following its suppression in Czechoslovakia, Marxist-humanism has been stifled in almost every country in Eastern Europe. It is virtually dead, for example, in Poland, where a wave of nationalistic anti-Semitism hounded both Jewish and non-Jewish intellectuals out of the Party and positions of influence. Even in Yugoslavia, which did permit some degree of freedom, Marxist-humanism no longer has much of a voice. Here there was an effort by the best scholars in Eastern Europe to re-read Marx and to find, particularly in his earlier writings, a humanism of both ideals and principles. It was used as a critique of Stalinism and a defense of democratic socialism. But at present the humanism of Marx the moralist has been supplanted by the orthodoxy of the Party.

Democracy without socialism is incomplete, Marxists insist. But socialism without democracy is a fraud. Is the Soviet Union—or indeed are any alleged socialist countries—as yet socialist? Although there has been a transfer of ownership and control of the means of production from one class to another, the workers do not control their own lives nor direct their own destinies. They not only do not control the factories in which they work, but are part of a vast bureaucratic industrial society and have merely exchanged employers. The conditions of work are as they were before, though there is less freedom in any elementary sense and there are no free trade unions with the recognized right to strike. Although power has been transferred to others, it is doubtful that it has been humanized.

Can socialism ever be achieved and can it be libertarian? Can one be both free and equal at the same time, democratic in economic *and* political terms? This question still has not been answered; in virtually no country in the world may a truly humanistic, democratic socialist society be said to exist—not in the communist regimes of Eastern Europe, which are under Soviet occupation and tutelage, nor in Cuba, which is under the control of the dictatorship of the Party, nor in China, where different forms of oppression exist. Communist societies are trying to mold the new man of the future; but who will educate the so-called educators? What guarantee is there that they will not destroy man in the effort to remake him? One bitter lesson to be learned is that one cannot enjoy economic democracy unless one has some measure of political democracy. The need for an *open* society has been demonstrated. What is essential is the existence of genuine civil liberties, of the legal right of opposition, of pluralistic political parties, of a free press and independent media of communication, and of voluntary associations. Without them a dominant class can rule with impunity. Without them a society stagnates. Only by releasing individuals and allowing them truly to participate in all of its institutions can a society become dynamic and progressive, and the common good and individual happiness be made possible. Anything short of this is a betrayal of the basic principles of humanism.

IV / Recent Disciples

THE NEW LEFT

Is the God that failed truly dead? Or is Marxism still the wave of the future? In many countries, particularly in the West, there has been a neo-Marxist revival, which goes by the name of the New Left so as to distinguish it from the errors of the Old Left. The New Left is already past middle-age, and a good deal of its influence and force is in disarray. Whether this is a temporary lull or the permanent decline of a fashion is difficult to say. We can now, however, examine the New Left with some historical perspective. Does it have a program that is new, that distinguishes it from other forms of Marxism?

New Leftists claimed to be aware of the betrayal of socialist-humanism by Stalinism and the Soviet state bureaucracy. They were prone to admit that socialism, as they conceived it, does not exist as yet anywhere in the world. But at the same time they berated liberalism in the West, and especially the United States, for having compromised humanistic principles, and for having defended the "corporate state," the "consumer society," the "military-industrial complex," a system of "imperialist exploitation" and "racism," which they said keeps a large section of the Third World under domination. They looked to "libertarian socialism" as a viable alternative.

The program of the New Left in many Western countries includes many conflicting tendencies. No clearly enunciated principles have been set forth; rather there is a generalized mood or attitude. The New Left emphasized action rather than thought, the deed rather than the word. Part of the movement was political-ideological and committed to a broad Marxist program: its heroes were Che Guevara and Castro, Ho Chi Minh and Mao, Herbert Marcuse and Frantz Fanon. Another part declared a cultural revolution, a rejection of the values of liberalism, capitalism, and bureaucratic communism; it was an effort to build a counterculture, a new life style, in which hair length, drugs, and sexual freedom played vital roles. It was both socialist in its political ideology and libertarian in its life style.

The New Left surprised the intellectual world; it perplexed and confounded the older generation. All sorts of explanations were offered to account for its emergence: the decay of capitalism, the decline of the professions, the results of a permissive society, the generation gap, and so on. The interpretation that the New Left itself offered was that contemporary youth had become alienated because of the final decay of the capitalist system. The consumer society is basically corrupt and hypocritical, it claimed, and young people had sensed this and were rebelling. This account maintained that capitalism is by its very nature imperialistic and racist and that it exploits colonial peoples (nonwhites) at home and abroad. Capitalism necessarily means that a large sector of the working force will be unemployed, with the economy in constant crisis; and the students are the new oppressed class of "lumpenproletariat," forced to stay out of the labor market because there are no jobs. They must become part of the new vanguard in alliance with the blacks and other nonwhites to overthrow the corrupt system and create a new one. The New Left at one point deviated widely from the orthodox Marxist view of how to bring about a revolution; for it denied workers a key role in the revolution, and tried to find a new base in an alliance between the students and the blacks. This strategy expressed a form of romanticism; the revolutionary students often were not of an oppressed class, but children of the affluent who enjoyed luxuries and privileges. To interpret the student movement in Marxist terms, therefore, as a problem of capitalism is an over-simplification. All technological-industrial societies today are in a crisis of change, and their youth sense the resulting dislocations. Similar strains have occurred in other parts of the world, whether capitalist or noncapitalist. The defects of modern life—imperialism, nationalism, ethnocentricism, and racism—transcend national and ideological frontiers. There is, however, a limited economic explanation that perhaps applies to student alienation—a kind of crisis of the professions. Those who revolted in the colleges and universities of the United States seemed to come predominantly from literature, philosophy and sociology departments, and less from the technological and scientific fields where there seemed to be a place for their talents.

Another explanation of student protest is the conflict between generations. Lewis Feuer in his book *The Conflict of Generations*[1] has argued that the revolt of sons against fathers is a constantly recurring feature of history. He also pointed out that student excesses have usually been followed by repression. There is a good deal of truth in Feuer's observations; he provides some explanation of why the students were rebelling. But while his thesis does not go far enough—there were other important causes, as we shall see—it also goes too far, for it has been shown that the ideological revolutionaries (if not the counterculture hippies) in many cases do not differ from their parents in political or moral values. As Kenneth Keniston pointed out, they are predominantly the children of liberals or leftists.[2] They had taken their parents at their word and were attempting to fulfill or realize many of their parents' aims and aspirations. Thus they were not necessarily rejecting the beliefs of their fathers but insisting upon their application. It is true that there are serious generational differences, especially evident in the counterculture and the use of drugs, but whether the generational hypothesis is sufficient by itself may be doubted.

[1] N. Y. Basic Books, 1969.
[2] Kenneth Keniston, *Young Radicals: Notes on Committed Youth*, N. Y., Harcourt, Brace and World, 1968.

Another explanation that has some merit concerns the degree of permissiveness in our society. Parents schooled in the years of John Dewey, Sigmund Freud, and Benjamin Spock are reluctant to apply excessive discipline to their children for fear of frustrating their creativity. There has been a tendency to permit children to enjoy a maximum of freedom to express themselves. This was undoubtedly a significant factor in some pampering of rebels: children are individuals; whatever they say has meaning and significance; therefore, we ought to listen to them. Related to the permissive syndrome is the adulation of youth which seems to pervade American culture. Youth is beautiful, the source and fountain of innocence and truth. What is newest or latest is best; the old worn-out models are to be discarded. Yet, granting the criticisms of permissiveness, it should be pointed out that children excessively repressed by their elders also tend to rebel against authority. The impulse to rebellion has many causes.

Religious Expression

There is another significant cause of rebellion that those close to the student movement have often noticed, but not often fully appreciated—its religious character. During its height, the movement was *basically a religious-moral phenomenon,* a thundering expression of a psychic hunger and need. This perhaps explains both its irrationality to those who reject it and its attraction for its partisans. The fact that "Jesus freaks," oriental meditation, and Asian cults now attract many of the former militants reinforces the religious hypothesis.

Anyone who observed the many young leftists on university campuses during the heyday of the protest movement must surely have been struck by their intense religious fervor. Apparently only the initiated could fully understand what it was all about. There were important signs to indicate who was the true believer and who was not: long hair, bizarre clothing, drugs, especially pot, rock music. To enter into one of the numerous mass meetings that were convened by the revolutionaries was especially revealing. One could not help feeling—much as an anthropologist would in recording the cultural behavior of an exotic tribe—that here was another culture at another time and in another place. The mass meetings were like the religious festivals of primitive cults and the revival meetings of fundamentalist Christian sects, full of excitement and emotion, saturated with piety and confessions. Apocalyptic rhetoric dominated the speeches; there was chanting and screaming. The mood was electric, fervent, hysterical; testimonials of devotion were made. At times, powerful symbolic slogans and incantations were introduced to call forth the faithful: "Power to the people!" evoked cheers of approval —all rose together, saluting with clenched fists. "Down with the pigs!" brought forth a response of frenzied rage. For the initiated there were two forces at work in the universe: the forces of darkness (capitalists, imperialists, renegades, administrators, pigs), and the forces of light (students, workers, blacks, revolutionaries). There was ambivalence about the world: a double response of love and hate, comradeship and vilification, affection and anger. Each of the faithful shared in a common vision which gave meaning and significance to his being. Thus Marxism, originally offered as a scientific analysis of a society and a hopeful method for social reconstruction, was again betrayed by its zealots, again transformed into a new religion, a new cult of the self-righteous.

One may only conjecture whether the New Left was merely a temporary aberration, provoked especially by outrage at the Vietnam war, or whether it will persist, perhaps developing new forms; whether, essentially, it is part of a larger historical tendency. History is made by men; what will happen will depend in part on what we do.

The traditional religions are rapidly dying, unable to adjust to the scientific-technological age; as a result there is a groping for new symbols, new values, new ideals by which men can live. The technological-bureaucratic societies that have developed in both capitalist and Marxist countries are similar: in both cases forms of alienation have emerged. It is in the face of a depersonalized, dehumanized existence that modern man has been seeking a new vision of meaning and truth. Perhaps the fury and passion of the religious revival may be explained by the fact that death as a category is omnipresent for modern man. For the first time he has had to contemplate the possible collective death of mankind. (George Wald, the Harvard scientist, has stated that the reason why the younger generation has often seemed irrational and desperate is perhaps that they have sensed that mankind has no future and that they were the generation that would not survive.) Thus the great scientific revolution of modern times has finally caught up with us. By means of the controlled use of scientific method we have been able to transform the surface of the globe and also napalm-bomb villages, pollute the atmosphere, trigger a population explosion, and create the horrendous possibility of nuclear disaster.

That this has resulted in a profound revulsion and turning away from the scientific world-view should not be a cause of wonder. Indeed, history has shown this sort of reaction is to be expected. Every generation that has had bold confidence in science and reason seems to be followed by one that finds serious limitations in naturalism. People generally seek to supplement reason, conceptualization, and logic with romanticism, mysticism, and idealism, with protests of feeling against thought. The artist, for example, responds to the scientist and rationalist with the criticism that he has left something out and that there needs to be a return to aesthetic appreciation of the immediacy of experience. There is truth in this claim: It is the *whole* man that is important, and emotion and intellect, theory and practice, philosophy and art, should be fused.

Yet in some periods the pendulum moves too far the other way and is then immobilized. Domination by irrationalism and neo-primitivism prevails. We may be entering a period characterized by such beliefs, at least for a significant minority. This has been especially manifest among the New Left and the counterculture, and by recent excursions into mysticism, astrology and the occult. It is hard to believe that the scientific-technological structure of modern life will be exorcised like a demon, especially in light of the marvels produced by modern science. Yet human affairs are often overwhelmed by the unthinkable.

The danger signals of such an event emerge when pathological religious attitudes predominate. This happened, for example, at the end of the Graeco-Roman humanistic era when Christianity prevailed. In recent times, there was the growth of fascism, a monstrous perversion that was prepared to devour the finest aspect of human culture. Fascism was a fanatic and confused ideological-religious movement, with all the pomp of a tribal cult. It attracted young people, particularly in Germany and Italy, and many intellectuals who allied themselves with the dregs of society to build a "New Order."

To force a strict analogy upon the threats of fascism, Marxism, and the New Left is one-sided and unfair. There are significant differences between Marxism and fascism; and the New Left, particularly in the United States, has in many ways made a genuine political-economic critique of modern society and a perceptive devaluation of our system of moral values. Indeed, at least in one sense the New Left has been quite humanistic—calling for a return to humane values and the fulfillment of the human potential—yet in another sense it has expressed a quasi-religious fanaticism reminiscent of the worst features of any religion, whether Christianity, Stalinism, or fascism. It has performed all the functions of religion, as these have previously been defined. We must keep in mind that it is not the content of the belief, but how it operates that characterizes something as religious.

There are at least two aspects to the religion of the New Left. First, it has an ideological character, with an affinity to Marxism in some distorted sense, which focuses on social and collective values. Second, it has a non-Marxist, non-ideological, countercultural aspect, which focuses on individual values and has a psychedelic dimension.

The New Left and Marxist Ideology

It is difficult to find a theory commonly espoused by the New Left; for it consciously eschews theory and emphasizes action, commitment, passion. Like a neo-primitive Christianity it rejects concept-playing, sterile formulas, theology. Mao, Debray, Marcuse, and Che are regarded as heroic figures, and in none of these writers, with the exception of Marcuse, is there a profound theoretical system. All, again with the exception of Marcuse, are primarily actors in history, rather than passive theoreticians. In reading the ideological literature of the New Left, one is struck by the absence of any really new concepts or theories. Generally, Marxism is used to provide the basic intellectual framework and Leninism in an extended sense is applied to the imperfect state of the world. There is, however, a practical relation to Marxism. The great question throughout seems to be how to apply Marxism to society, how to destroy capitalism, how to bring about socialism.

The devotees of the New Left are troubled by the fact that though

Marxism has been preached for a century in many countries of the West, its prophecy has not been fulfilled. Socialism has captivated large sections of the intelligentsia and of the general population, yet it has not been implemented. Are we never going to obtain the promises of a socialist society? Not by the slow processes of democracy, nor by passive methods of compromise, say the New Leftists. Social democrats have talked and talked about the evolution of socialism, especially in the advanced industrial societies, which seem no closer to realizing the dream than they were at the turn of the century. (One reason, no doubt, is that workers now enjoy a higher standard of living.) There is a mood of desperation; it is time for decisive action, we are told, not theory or talk. We must act now, seize the time. The Stalinist state-oriented bureaucratic societies where Marxist revolutions have occurred—the bourgeoisie destroyed and the means of production nationalized—have also, we are told, betrayed the original promise of socialism; in its place have come repressive dictatorships. Therefore, the formulas of the Party communists in totalitarian communist societies, as well as those of the socialists in the democratic capitalist societies, must be abandoned.

To replace these failures, New Leftists looked to the dynamic of the underdeveloped countries of the world which have added a new dimension to revolutionary development since World War II. Mao, Ho, Che, and Castro seemed to them to have abandoned compromise and to be taking new paths to build socialism, which itself remains as the only hope of mankind. Believing that the large Third World of nonwhite peoples is exploited by industrial capitalist powers, which use them to import raw materials and to export manufactured goods, the New Left here applied Leninism to their analysis of the situation. Capitalism, it is said, is still, and will always be, colonialism.

All political myths must have *some* basis in reality if they are widely believed, and there clearly is some truth in the indictment of capitalist imperialism. Yet claims of truth can be extended into fantasy, and this is what has happened with the New Left's imperialistic bugaboo. After World War II, in the light of liberal and socialist criticism and native nationalist movements, the major colonial powers—especially Britain, France, Belgium, and Holland—largely withdrew from their vast empires. Large areas of the underdeveloped countries in Asia and Africa were given autonomy and independence. Far from having expanded, colonialism in its classic sense has retreated. It is true that the United States after World War II (at the behest of liberals and leftists and in *opposition* to conservative political and corporate managers, who were isolationists) entered into an expanded leadership role. I surely do not wish by these comments to defend all the contradictions and blunders of subsequent American foreign policy. Its political-economic-military role has been exaggerated and needs to be reappraised; for it has had a considerable drain on the political order and economy. Yet economic investments and trade overseas are only a very small part of the total capital investments or gross national product of the United States. Moreover, part of the investment and aid was made at the request of governments for economic and military assistance and for help in development. While it is true that many capitalist countries have investments overseas, they have often helped to build up indigenous industries. But it is a two-way street; foreign capital is also heavily invested in the United States by Europe and Japan, among others. If all foreign investments were withdrawn from these areas, their development would be drastically impaired if not destroyed. (These remarks should not, of course, be construed as condoning high profits and exploitation.) The Soviet Union has also exported military and economic aid to Cuba, Egypt, India, and many other countries; and it has behaved as badly as other great powers in Eastern Europe and elsewhere. The complaints of China, Yugoslavia, Hungary, and Czechoslovakia bear witness. The phenomenon of great power and influence is apparently independent of whether a nation-state happens to be capitalist or socialist.

It cannot be denied that American foreign policy has made some terrible blunders. It has supported corrupt military regimes (Spain, Pakistan, Greece, Vietnam), but it has also supported socialist regimes (Yugoslavia, Rumania, and India). There are no black and white principles that operate on the international level, in a world of separate, often antagonistic, competing, and self-interested sovereign powers, where it is the balance of power that in the last analysis always seems to be decisive. We may deplore this on moral grounds, but military power will continue to play a major role in the foreign policies of nations until some system of world government can develop. The point is that foreign policy has been turned into an area for competing religious dogmas. For the New Left the enemy is always capitalist and colonial imperialism; all venom and anger must be heaped upon the conspiracy of these devils and, the litany reads, true peace and justice will not prevail until capitalism is vanquished.

A movement for national liberation against repressive regimes and foreign intervention may be defended on rational grounds, provided it is related to a movement for world government. The trouble is that the movement for national liberation in some parts of the world has become the holy crusade of a new kind of fanatic cult, which has inspired not only the people directly involved but sympathetic supporters in other countries as well.

THE NEW RELIGION: MAO, CHE, CASTRO, DEBRAY

The Third World emerged at the center of the New Left's ideological struggle. Maoism was hailed as the wave of the future; like the other philosophies we have examined, it had many religious connotations. Mao claimed to be a Leninist and a Stalinist—indeed, the only true one. Ideologically, Maoism will brook no compromise with revisionism or deviationism. It will not allow bureaucracy to overlay the authentic Marxist creed with sterile formulations. It expresses a deep-felt commitment to the cause. There is a revealing passage in the writings of Mao in which the need to bind the individual to the Party and its cause is made transparently clear; note the religious component: "A communist should be frank, faithful and active," says Mao, "looking upon the interests of the revolution as his very life and subordinating his personal interests to those of the revolution." He should, he says, "always and everywhere adhere to correct principles and wage a tireless struggle against all incorrect ideas and actions, so as to consolidate the collective life of the Party and strengthen the ties between the Party and the masses." And he concludes, "he should be more concerned about the Party and the masses than about the individual; and more concerned about others than about himself. Only thus can he be considered a communist."[3]

In his famous essay "On Contradiction" Mao reveals the powerful

---

[3] From "Combat Liberalism," 1937. Reprinted in Arthur P. Mendel, *Essential works of Marxism, op. cit.*, p. 516.

hold that the Marxist-Hegelian dialectic has on his life: "The law of the contradiction in things," he writes, "that is, the law of the unity of opposites, is the basic law of nature and society and therefore also the basic law of thought." He goes on: "If, after study, we have really understood the essential points mentioned above, we shall be able to smash those doctrinaire ideas which run counter to the basic principles of Marxism-Leninism and are detrimental to our revolutionary cause, and also enable our experienced comrades to systematize their experiences so as to impart to them the character of principle. . ."[4]

For Mao, theoretical principles mean little until they are put into action. They must stimulate psychological actuation; commitment and dedication must become internalized principles of motivation so that they can have a social impact. The individual is called upon to sacrifice everything for the Faith. The similarity to Christianity here is evident; the so-called cultural revolution in China seemed to give full encouragement to religious idolatry. In light of this, the efforts by Mao and Chou En-lai to work out with Nixon and Kissinger a detente with the U. S. came as a blow to the religious faithful, as inexplicable as Stalin's willingness to ally with Hitler on the eve of World War II. Fear of the Russians was probably a major factor in China's decision; but, whatever the causes, it has deflated (perhaps only temporarily) the crusade in other parts of the world.

While Maoism cherished statutes of the dead apostles Lenin and Stalin, Che Guevara represented a new communist martyr whom the most extreme New Leftists adored. According to John Gerassi, who has edited Guevara's writings, Che was a romantic: "He lived and died for others—for a better world, a world where people can really love, instead of just 'coming to terms'; just compromising." "That is why," says Gerassi, "Che is so popular among young America. That is why he is not dead."[5]

Che Guevara proclaims: "Revolutionary conduct is the mirror of revolutionary faith, and when someone calls himself a revolutionary

---

[4] From *Mao Tse-tung, An Anthology of His Writings,* ed. Anne Fremantle, N. Y., The New American Library, 1962, pp. 240-41.
[5] *Venceremos! The Speeches and Writings of Che Guevara,* N. Y., Simon and Schuster, 1968, p. xix.

and does not act as one, he can be nothing more than heretical."[6]
He focuses on "the capacity for sacrifice and says that he is "oriented
toward the future."[7] "The revolutionary's backbone is the vision of
the luminous future of socialist society."[8] The symbols of the young
communist are "study, work, and the rifle";[9] enthusiasm itself is not
enough, unless there is an organization to carry this forward. So inspired was Guevara that he took his mission in life to be to carry the
revolution to other parts of the world, and was eventually killed in
Bolivia leading a small band of guerrillas in the noble cause.

Another of the New Left's mythic figures, Regis Debray, elabor-
ated upon the Maoist-Guevara approach and the need for a new
guerrilla strategy. Arrested in Bolivia after the death of Che Guevara
and charged with aiding the insurrectionists, he reflected upon the
coming struggle in Latin America and the Third World. The religious
connotations of this crusade are unmistakable. There must be a new
strategy, he says, because one cannot depend simply upon the Communist Party, and surely not on peaceful methods of social change.
For him, the Cuban revolution proves that the bourgeois state can
be overthrown only by an armed struggle. But "there can be no revolution," he maintains, quoting Castro, "without a vanguard, tena-
ciously committed to its goals." The old Communist Party is not
sufficient. The new strategy requires that the vanguard be transformed into an army: "The political and military are not separate,
but form one organic whole, consisting of the people's army, whose
nucleus is the guerrilla army. The guerrilla force is the party in em-
bryo."[10]

There must be no divorce between Marxist theory and revolutionary practice; they must be unified. The new organization is so devoted to military operations as its first line of attack that there must be
a reconstitution, which "requires the temporary suspension of 'internal' party democracy and the temporary abolition of the principles
of democratic centralism which guarantee it . . . party discipline be-

[6] *Ibid.*, p. 130.
[7] *Ibid.*, p. 207.
[8] *Ibid.*, p. 209.
[9] *Ibid.*, p. 210.
[10] Regis Debray, *Revolution in the Revolution: Armed Struggle and Political Struggle in Latin America*, N. Y., Grove Press, 1967, p. 106.

comes military discipline."[11] According to Debray, the guerrilla forces cannot tolerate any fundamental duality of powers, and he quotes Che Guevara in urging that the military and political leaders be "united, if possible, in one person."[12]

The quotations from Debray show how Leninist doctrine has actually been applied to the revolutionary situation and also how any means—including the abrogation of democracy—will be invoked if necessary to achieve victory over bourgeois society. But more, there emerges a kind of military psychology which dominates the movement. The revolutionary struggle sweeps the individual into its fold and gives his life meaning and purpose. "The first law of guerrilla life," says Debray, "is that no one survives it alone." Indeed, "the group's interest is the interest of each one, and vice versa." And "to live and conquer is to live and conquer all together."[13] "Revolutionaries," he observes, "make revolutionary civil wars; but to an even greater extent it is revolutionary civil war that makes revolutionaries."[14]

We see here a new drama of resurrection in which both the individual and the group are unified in fire, working for the utopian future. Debray even feels called upon to use religious symbolism to describe the kind of mystical relation of the revolutionary to the Revolution:

> Here the political world is abruptly made flesh. The revolutionary ideal emerges from the gray shadow of formula and acquires substance in the full light of day. This transubstantiation comes as a surprise, and when those who have experienced it want to describe it—in China, in Vietnam, in Cuba, in many places—they resort not to words but to exclamation.[15]

Does not this explain the power of the guerrilla in places such as Vietnam where, opposed by the powerful American army with its overwhelmingly massive fire power, the guerrillas were able to succeed? How would this be possible, but for the mystical-religious

[11] *Ibid.*, p. 103.
[12] *Ibid.*, p. 107.
[13] *Ibid.*, p. 110.
[14] *Ibid.*, p. 111.
[15] *Ibid.*, p. 112.

power of the religious-ideological ideal, which becomes the very principle of being for the combatant fighting for his vision of a new world? A great danger which those who are opposed to religious fanaticism, whether theistic or revolutionary, must recognize is that religious systems often thrive when they are persecuted; martyrs are of course created by those who seek to stamp them out. It is the struggle itself that gives strength, dedication, and devotion when they might otherwise be absent. The Christian's being thrown to the lions by the Romans only redoubled the efforts of his fellow believers, and the communist's being pitched in battle against his oppressor only causes him to quicken his revolutionary faith and confirms his hatred of the existing regime. Truth does not come out of the muzzle of a gun, but moral resolve often does. To force a movement of true believers underground one day is to risk the danger that they will surface the next—with added power. Lenin and Stalin were conspirators hounded by the Czarist police, much the same as Jesus and Paul were hounded by the authorities centuries before them. Prisons are often hothouses for new religious fervors.

Fidel Castro was puzzled by the intensity of commitment that he observed among his guerrilla fighters in the Sierra Maestra:

> The renovating spirit, the longing for collective excellence, the awareness of a higher destiny are in full flower. . . . Where did they acquire so much ability, astuteness, courage, self-sacrifice? No one knows! It is almost a mystery! They organize themselves all alone, spontaneously! When weary animals drop to the ground, unable to go further, men appear from all directions and carry the goods. Force cannot defeat them . . . the people are aware of it and are daily more aware of their own growing strength.[16]

Debray agrees. The militants, he says, are fighters, aggressive, resolute, responsible. What brought them to the mountain was "the awareness of a historic necessity."[17]

That people of the New Left in other countries are inspired by the rhetoric of the guerrillas, that their behavior seems so irrational, emotional, recalcitrant, that they are willing to use any kind of terroristic

---

[16] From Fidel Castro's last letter to Frank Pais, written in the Sierra Maestra, July 21, 1957, and quoted in Debray, *op. cit.*, p. 113.
[17] *Ibid.*, p. 113.

tactics to further their goals—none of this should seem surprising when one considers the religious imperative behind their quest. They are not reluctant warriors, but militant crusaders—wholly committed to the prophecies of their bible.

It is possible that this discussion has placed undue stress on what many observers have called a "lunatic fringe." It is, of course, true that only a minority of the New Left accepted an extremely militant version of neo-Marxism; yet this may be taken as a symptom of other possibilities. Should the New Left, the thrust of which has declined, finally disappear, especially in the West, other religious cults are waiting in the wings—though perhaps without the blessings of the intellectuals: the Jesus freaks, Krishna people, transcendental meditators, purveyors of witchcraft and astrology, and so forth. It is hardly possible to argue with true believers, whether Jehovah's Witnesses, Jesus freaks, Muslims, Stalinists, Maoists, or New Leftists. One can only hope to prevent them from imposing their will on others.

Disregard of historical experience, failure to see things in perspective, inability to make balanced judgments, are all signs of religious neurosis; and the willingness to use any means to achieve one's ends is the sickness of a moralist gone mad. Only the most fanatic religions are capable of bringing out the worst, as well as the best, in men; along with courage and heroism, sympathy and love, sacrifice and cooperation, they preach an amorality that glorifies hatred and intolerance. In the New Left, we have seen a graphic illustration of this paradox. While some New Leftists are genuine pacifists, others have glorified force and violence as harbingers of a higher morality. Violence is sometimes necessary in human life—when all other means fail, when the good to be gained is far greater than the evils to be suffered. But violence should be only a last resort, based upon a careful and deliberate calculation of consequences, for it may destroy the very ends one wishes to achieve.

A passionate ideologist is all too prone to justify violence if it fits his strategy. An unbeliever, on the contrary, can be committed to the ideal of an open society and be willing to tolerate other religious points of view, however mistaken they may seem to him— so long, that is, as they do not interfere with the expressions or rights of others. Some religions, unlike neo-Marxism, have been far less dangerous and far more considerate of the wishes of others. The danger of many religious believers is not that their religion offers hope to the weary—if that is what they need, let them have their myths—but that they attempt to convert other souls by any means at their disposal. How are we to be saved from the saved, especially when they resort to revolutionary tactics?

Some say that the New Left has been defeated. Certainly it was in part a creature of the mass media, and the young are now bored with it, but there are other explanations for its eclipse: Student excesses resulted in penalties, police crackdowns. Many idealistic students became dismayed when they saw that the man in the street, particularly the worker, was hostile toward them and their methods; that bombing a building might mean suspension or expulsion from a university, possibly even arrest and indictment. The heady days of Daniel Bendit-Cohn and of Berkeley and Columbia gradually dissipated in the face of widespread public criticism. Herbert Marcuse in *Counter-Revolution and Revolt*[18] argues that the retreat of the New Left is only a phase of reflection, that new strategies and tactics will be adopted for the long march to revolution. Whether he is correct remains to be seen. If the student movement has had its ups and downs, Marxism as a world-wide phenomenon still has vitality. The New Left perhaps is only the most passionate and vocal expression of a deeper and more lasting current.

Will religious Marxism be turned back? If it is, it may be because of internecine warfare. The intense conflict between Soviet and Chinese Marxism is ideological and nationalistic. Its continuation can have serious repercussions on the world-wide Marxist movement. No one can predict what will happen. Paralleling the outcome of theological controversies between Protestants and Catholics, Mohammedans and Hindus, communism may degenerate into warring sects. Moreover, war between the Soviet Union and China, aside from the great suffering it would cause, would have an incalculable impact on the world-wide communist movement, for it would explode a romantic myth that wars are only inspired by capitalist powers. On the other hand, if Russian neo-Stalinists were one day to assume power in China and were able to work out a rapprochement between Mos-

[18] Boston, Beacon Press, 1972.

cow and Peking, the Marxist push forward could again become massive. This would not be the inevitable result of historical forces—only the true disciple seriously believes that—but the result of the attraction and fire of a religious appeal combined with the power of military and economic forces.

If an authoritarian and fanatic version of Marxism is not to overwhelm the world, a positive attitude must fill the vacuum. This must be a democratic humanism, which can use the best of Marxist socialism, but combine it with reason, freedom, and democracy.

THE COUNTER-CULTURE AND A NEW MORALITY

Radical critics will no doubt complain that the above analysis is unfair. Constructive contributions have indeed been made by present-day radicalism. Critiques of the shortcomings, hypocrisies, and injustices of our society are necessary for dealing with the smug complacency that values nominal Christianity, blind anti-communism, the CIA and FBI, Madison Avenue, moon rocketry, racism, ghetto life, and cherry pie. The New Left was concerned with defending peace and protesting the U. S. involvement in Vietnam, demanded a reordering of national priorities, objected to the domination of society by corporate interests, and asked for socialization. It wished to gain equality of opportunity for blacks and other disadvantaged groups, for women, the poor, homosexuals, and prisoners; it demanded a radical restructuring of the university and insisted that students be treated as human beings, and that the system be relevant to the society at large. The movement included liberals who wished to work within the system in order to achieve peaceful change as well as radicals and revolutionaries who were committed to violence. Perhaps, then, much of the New Left is basically part of the profound moral upheaval that is occurring in all parts of the world; perhaps the emergence of the counter-culture is a sign that the old values are being overthrown and that new ones are emerging. Surely there are new directions to be taken, other forms of consciousness to be developed. It is the moral rather than the political or economic revolution that is crucial in the new society that people wish to build in the new age.

Contemporary man has various options. He may be tempted by the blandishments of religious fanaticism or utter nihilism. Nietszche defined "nihilism" as a state of mind in which "everything is permitted." If this were our disposition, we could do whatever we wanted and nothing would really be worth anything. Nihilism constantly threatens man, particularly during times of great frustration and social change. Its ascendancy, like that of religious orthodoxy, would mean the destruction of the true humanist spirit, for it invalidates the possibility of constructive change.

The so-called counter-culture is a bizarre blend of religiosity and nihilism. Simply turning away from what is does not guarantee something better. *Counter*-culture need not mean an alternative culture; it can be *anti*-culture and *contra* the true, good, and beautiful. Fascism in a sense was also counter-culture, for it was against many cherished and enduring values of Western civilization and it substituted, for reason and civility, new forms of action, commitment, and passion. An anti-intellectual counter-culture that preaches violence, hatred, and free drugs is hardly the model for a new civilization. The option is not to herald counter-culture but to construct a *new* culture.

The so-called counter-culture began with the positive premise that moral values are *human,* not supernatural, that they should not be imposed by archaic moral or social traditions, and that they should not be forfeited to an increasingly depersonalized organizational-technological society. Our complex culture contains vestiges of formal structures and rules derived from earlier epochs which, when forced on us, stultifies many potential human qualities. Accordingly, we need to be freed from such oppression. The counter-culture made a big issue of the social pressures restricting such things as hair and dress styles, free drugs, free sex, and other standards of conformity.

The counter-culture made another point: Because of the kind of society that stresses competition and conflict, individuals are often cut off from others. Contemporary society commercializes relationships and depersonalizes individuality. Hucksters and advertisers judge human worth financially, consider people to be mere commodities, to be used, bartered, exchanged. But men are not objects; they are subjects, with dignity and value, and should be appreciated. We need to restore a sense of fraternity and brotherhood, to become capable of genuinely shared experience and cooperation. Only by belonging to some community can humans discover common values. By learning to appreciate the needs of others, we can expand our store of truth and beauty, and develop values of solidarity and communality.

The counter-culture recognized the anti-libertarian and anti-communitarian tendencies of modern life; and it wished to restore freedom and sociality. The Port Huron statement of the Students for a Democratic Society, published in 1962 at the beginning of the student movement, emphasized democratic and humanistic values and sought to create a good society. The statement had inspiring things to say about the kinds of values that ought to be achieved:

> We regard *men* as infinitely precious and possessed of unfulfilled capacities for reason, freedom and love . . . We oppose the depersonalization that reduces human beings to the status of things—if anything, the brutalities of the twentieth century teach that means and ends are intimately related . . . . Men have unrealized potential for self-cultivation, self-direction, self-understanding and creativity . . . The goal of man and society should be human independence . . . . a concern . . . . with finding a meaning in life that is personally authentic . . . *Human relationships* should involve fraternity and honesty . . . We would replace power rooted in possession, privilege, or circumstance by power and uniqueness rooted in love, reflectiveness, reason, and creativity.[19]

How tragic it is that these aims were debased by certain tendencies within the counter-culture; for in an effort to be liberated from authoritarian structures, counter-culturists often abandoned the conditions of reason and self-imposed responsibility that are essential to a free man; and in an effort to find a framework for common human values, the virtues of the commune brought back a set of authoritarian principles imposed from without.

The principle of libertarianism urges that individuals be freed as far as possible from social restrictions. Law should not regulate morality; hence, all legal restrictions preventing people from expressing their values should be removed. It is unfortunate, however, that the principle of libertarianism has been appealed to by the young for a cause like the legalization of marijuana and drug use. It is paradoxical that for some this should have become the great social issue. Yet this points again toward current religious tendencies. The counterculture's insistence upon the right of individuals to pursue drug ex-

[19] *The New Left: A Documented History,* ed. by Massimo Teodori, Indianapolis, Bobbs-Merrill Co., 1969, pp. 166-67.

periments without social limitations is obviously rooted in a quest for hedonic pleasure and thrills, but it also signals a mystical drive to certain kinds of expanded awareness.

The counter-culture also expressed a new attitude toward work, a new view of sex and the sexual revolution, sympathy with anarchism, despair with reason, science and technology, flirtation with the irrational, emphasis on the commune in opposition to the individual, a desire to contribute to the greening of a society made bleak by industrialization and technology. It has some decidedly negative as well as positive aspects. It may bring no culture, but mainly a breakdown of order, moderation, and reason without which civilized society is not possible. The permissive society may become the chaotic one. What we want is tolerance for different styles of life; not a breakdown of civilized life.

Having explored various unsuccessful ways of dealing with the contemporary condition, we return to the question with which we began: can man, freed from a religious or ideological morality, construct a new life with purpose and courage, based upon a realistic appraisal of both the limitations and the potentialities of man? Can he build a life enriched by pleasure and creativity, receptive to feeling, yet rational and concerned with social justice and well-being?

I shall now turn directly to these decisive issues. It is time to ask: Is an authentic humanism possible? If so, what would it entail?

Part Two / The Humanist Response

V / The Meaning of Life

ETHICS MINUS GOD

Does life have genuine meaning for one who rejects supernatural mythology (or Marxist ideology)? Can one realize a significant life if he abandons faith in immortality or providence? Is life tragic because it is finite? Since death surely awaits everyone, is life therefore absurd? (In answer, religious Marxism seeks to reinvest the cosmic void with historical purpose: Mankind is larger than any one individual and provides the individual with a beloved cause.) Faced with this existential dilemma, man cries out, "Why live?" Can we be happy? Is there a basis for moral conduct? What can we do if God is dead, if there is no immortal soul, and if there is no purpose imminent in nature?

It is important that we focus on the so-called problem of the meaning of life as it is posed by the theist. (The humanist at least shares with the Marxist the assumption that life is worth living.) In answer

85

to the theist, we may say that the existential question as framed by him is mistaken. We should not grant to the religious believer the validity of his challenge. Instead we should ask whether life is really meaningful for *him*. Does he not deceive himself by posing the theo-logical-existential paradox and by assuming that only a "broader" purpose can save him? Is it not the theist who squanders life? In what sense would life be worthwhile if God existed, if the universe had a divine purpose—and given the existence of "evil"?

The conception of an omnipotent God connotes the correlative notion of helpless creatures. "Man's chief end," admonishes the Scottish shorter catechism, "is to glorify God and enjoy him for ever and ever." What kind of life can be said to be significant if we are totally dependent upon this God for our existence and sustenance? The relationship of creator to created is analogous to that of master to slave. The religious picture of the universe is akin to a model prison, wherein inmates are beholden to the warden for their daily bread and their highest duty is to praise and supplicate him for life. The immortality myth warns that if we do not pledge allegiance to His will, we shall suffer damnation. Is not the life of an independent free man to be preferred to one of eternal bondage?

No, replies the believer to these skeptical questions. God promises eternal salvation, not oppression, for the elect. But upon what condition? As Bertrand Russell has said, to sing hymns in praise of Him and hold hands throughout all eternity would be sheer boredom. What of the lusts of the body, the joys of the flesh, the excitement and turmoil of pleasure and passion—will these be vanquished in the immortal life? For the free man, Hell could not be worse.

The religious believer insists that man is free; for he is created in God's image, capable of choosing between good and evil. The rub, however, is that only if he chooses to obey his master will he be rewarded with immortal life. But the problem of evil turns this eternal drama into divine comedy: God entrusted me with the power and freedom of choice, yet He will punish me if I stray from Him. Why did He not program me during the act of creation, so that I could not avoid knowing Him and following His guidelines. Since it is He who created me, why does He condemn me for satisfying my natural inclinations, which He implanted in me? Why does He permit suffer-ing and pain, torment and tragedy, disease and strife, war and plunder, conflict and chaos? In order to test us, responds the theist. But why the necessity of the trial, with so much apparent vindictiveness? To punish us for the sins we have committed. If this is the case, why punish the innocent? Why cut down the seeming paragons of virtue, the valiant and the noble? For the sins they have committed but may be unaware of? Why visit pain and torment upon infants and children—as in cancer or accident? Are they paying for the sins of their parents? If so, is this not a morality of collective guilt? (And what if the children are orphans!) One who believes in reincarnation may attempt to rescue the case by insisting on a prior existence. Possibly children are made to pay for the sins that they have committed in an earlier life, though as an ill child writhes and cries out, he does not remember those prior existences—as Caligula or Hitler—for which he now suffers.

The rationalization continues: Perhaps evil is due to man's omission, not God's commission. Man should discover a cure for cancer, for example, or learn to stop floods. But if God is all-powerful, why doesn't He intervene in cooperative venture? There is no natural evil, say some theists, attempting to resolve the problem; the only evil is "moral evil," they assert, the evil of man, not God. But the inescapable inference is that God permits evil. Why does He not stamp it out? Why should not God be merciful and loving rather than legalistic and moralistic? Is He, as Hume suggests, like us: merely limited in power? Then why worship another finite being?

Some theists insist that evil may only be an illusion, and that from a larger perspective what appears to be evil may turn out in the end to be good. In the total divine plan, pain and suffering need not be bad. Why is not the converse true? From the larger point of view what appears to be good may also be only an illusion, and everything in the end irredeemably evil.

Thus the believer has woven a fanciful fabric of mythological imagination in order to soothe his fear of death and to comfort those who share his anxiety. His is an *ad hoc* rationalization professing to settle his doubt; but it is ridden with loopholes more puzzling than the universe we encounter in everyday life.

Believers finally concede that there are things—from The Book of Job down to the present—beyond human understanding, such as the paradox of free will versus determinism and the problem of evil. Unable to resolve the contradictions, they end up in simple confessions of faith.

Should we not rather be prepared to deal with life as we find it—full of sorrow, death, pain, and failure, but also pregnant with possibilities?

But, insists the believer, man cannot be happy if he knows that he is going to die and that the universe for him possesses no larger purpose. What is happiness? Does it involve acquiescence to another, dependence on a greater being, religious faith and devotion, credulity and piety? Why is religious masochism a form of bliss? It may release us from torment and anxiety, but it involves flight from the full realization of our powers. Not only, therefore, does religious theism fail to give life "meaning," it fails as a source of happiness. More often than not it has exaggerated the pathology of fear, the anxiety of punishment, the dread of death and of the unknown.

The believer is tormented by his overextended sense of sin and guilt, torn by a struggle between natural biological impulses and repressive divine commandments. Can a religious believer who submits to a doctrine of sin truly be happy? For the humanist the great folly is to squander his life, to miss what it affords, not to play it out. The cemeteries are filled with corpses who bartered their souls in anticipation of promises that were never fulfilled.

But can one really be "moral," remonstrates the theist, without religious belief? Are we capable of developing "moral virtues" and a sense of responsibility without a belief in God as a presupposition of morality?

The answers here in part depend upon what is meant by the term "moral." Morality for the believer requires the existence of a faith state, a pious appreciation of God's redemptive power. This entails the "virtues" of acquiescence and obedience, as well as the suppression of our natural biological desires, including our appreciation of sexuality, and even some degree of self-hate. We may deny, however, that many of the so-called "moral virtues" of traditional theism are either moral or virtuous. The highest virtues are in man's existing for himself; self-interest, self-respect, pride, some element of self-centeredness are essential components of morality, which in the last analysis focuses on happiness. This being the case it is possible to be "moral" without belief in God.

But, asks the theist, if God is dead, is not *everything* permissible? Would man not be rapacious and misuse his fellow creatures? How, without God, can we guarantee charity and justice? The brotherhood of man presupposes a divine conception of individual dignity based upon the fatherhood of God. To abandon this postulate of the moral life would be to reduce men to hunter and prey in every form of barbarism.

Basically, these are empirical questions. There is no logical connection between the fatherhood of God and the brotherhood of man. A hierarchical church has defended an unequal society with strict social class and privilege. Moral sympathy is not dependent upon theistic belief. The Crusades and the Inquisition, the massacre of the Huguenots, the Moslem-Hindu slaughter in modern times, the Catholic-Protestant battles, as in Northern Ireland, are among the cruelties perpetrated by theists. Moreover, belief in God often deflects a concern for one's fellow men to supernatural goals; faith supersedes charity. If one's interest is the after-life, then there is a temptation for some—but surely not all—to render unto Caesar the things that are Caesar's. Churches have had little difficulty in suppressing progress and revolution. Franco and Salazar were true believers, as have been those in power in authoritarian regimes in South Africa, Greece, Portugal, and Pakistan. Religious devotion is no guarantee of moral devotion. Rather, there is good evidence that moral concern is autonomous and rooted in independent phenomenological experience. The history of mankind demonstrates that atheists, agnostics, and skeptics have been as moved by moral consideration for others as have believers. Marx, Engels, Russell, Mill, Dewey, and Sartre have had deep and abiding moral interests in the good of mankind and have not depended upon religious faith to bolster their morality. On the contrary, they have demonstrated that morality grounded in human experience and reason is a far more reliable guide to conduct.

IS LIFE WORTH LIVING?

There are other sources of despair. I have in mind the "existential plight" caused by life's exasperating and sometimes tragic difficulties, failures, and conflicts. There are moments when everything seems pointless, we wish to abandon all of our commitments, we may even contemplate suicide—profound crises of self-doubt and frustration. We may ask: Why beat one's head against a stone wall? What's the use?

At some point in life many of us have suspended desires, interests, and ideals: the death of a loved one, a cherished friend or relative, intense personal suffering, a disease, defeat of one's country, failure, deception uncovered, injustice perpetrated. The young burdened with the choice of a career; the middle-aged facing divorce or financial ruin; the old enduring the pangs of loneliness—all know moments of desperation.

Yet in spite of adversities and frustrations, the humanist maintains as his first principle that life is worth living, at least that it can be found to have worth. Can one demonstrate why the principle ought to prevail? Why express the courage to be? Why not die? Why life instead of death? If we are all going to die one day, why defer the inevitable? Why stave it off, why not *now*?

One cannot "prove" that life ought to exist, or that a universe with sentient beings is a better place than one without them. The universe is neutral, indifferent to man's existential yearnings. But we instinctively discover life, experience its throb, its excitement, its attraction. Life is there to be lived, enjoyed, suffered, and endured.

We must therefore rely on ourselves and distinguish two major, though distinct, questions. The first is epistemological, and the second psychological. Epistemologically, one may ask, can we "demonstrate" the basic principle of humanist morality, that is, that life is worthwhile? As his first principle, the theist adopts belief in a divine order beyond empirical confirmation or proof, which is in the last analysis a leap of faith. Does the first principle of humanism rest upon equal footing? In a crucial sense, my answer is No. For life is found; it is encountered; it is real. It needs no proof of its existence, as does an unknown and unseen divinity. The question is not: Does life exist? This is known as intimately and forcefully as anything in our universe of experience. The question rather is normative: *Ought* life to exist? This first principle does not make a descriptive claim; it is prescriptive and directive.

There are different kinds of first principles. They are not all of the same logical order; nor do they function in the same way. There are first principles that assert actual truth claims about the universe: for example, the assertion that God exists, or that determinism is real, or that the dialectic is operative in history. All of these principles have to be judged by the requirements of evidence and logic. Those that cannot provide sufficient grounds of support fail. A normative principle, as distinct from a descriptive assertion, is a guide for future conduct. It does not talk about the world in descriptive or explanatory terms. It lays down recommendations for us to follow, values to uphold, ideals to live by.

It is no doubt true that the epistemological principles of deductive logic, which provide for clarity in inference and thought, and of inductive science, which apply to the criteria for weighing evidential claims, function in one sense, prescriptively; for they provide guidelines for clarity and truth. In the last analysis they are justified pragmatically: do they assist in the course of inquiry? But still these are not truth claims of the same order as the God claim; for they are not attributing properties to the world. (If the theist were willing to abandon any descriptive claims about the universe, then "God exists" would be a normative principle, indicating moral imperatives for man. Such an ethical interpretation of theism would not suffer the objections that classical transcendental supernaturalism has. The major issue then would be the status of its moral principles, and whether they are viable.)

Theistic descriptive claims are bad answers to bad questions, such as: "Why in the universe at large should organic matter exist?" This makes no more sense than asking why things exist in the inanimate world. "Why ought there to be anything at all in the universe?" is a meaningless question, though no doubt for the religious consciousness a poignant one. The demand for an explanation of "Being in general" or for an answer to the "riddle of the universe" is inevitably elusive, because there is no such thing as "Being in general." There are a multiplicity of beings that may be said to exist—objects, organisms, persons. These entities are encountered in experience and may be submitted to analysis since they have discernible properties. The question *why* they exist with the properties they have, may be accounted for scientifically; they may be explained in causal terms, as having evolved in nature and as conditioned by natural laws. To ask *"why* Being in general?" on the contrary is both fruitless and pointless. To posit God as the alleged ground of Being does not advance inquiry. We can always ask why He exists. There are limits to genuine explanation, and certain kinds of questions and answers are beyond the range of intelligibility. The universe *is,* in a distributive way; that is, there are particular things. These we may encounter and describe in experience. Similarly, the question "Why should there be life in general?" can only be treated empirically. Any response would be in terms of known physical, chemical and biological principles. Life comes into being in our solar system and elsewhere when certain physical-chemical conditions are present.

The question that is sometimes raised in moments of existential despair is "Why should I exist?" or in recent decades, because of the threat of nuclear holocaust, "Why should the human race exist?" or still further, in consideration of ecological destruction, "Why should life on earth exist?" We have no guarantee, of course, that any forms of life will persist. Indeed, there is some probability that life on our planet may in some distant future become extinct, and this applies to the human race as well, unless by ingenuity and daring man can populate other portions of the universe. There is no *a priori* guarantee of eternal survival.

Whether or not the race of mankind continues indefinitely, however, an individual cannot persist forever. Thus the question "why" applies here most appropriately. "Why ought I to live?" "Can I prove that my life is better than my death?" ask the nihilist and skeptic in a mood of despondency. The answer should be apparent by now. One cannot prove that he ought to; all such proofs are deductive. From certain assumed premises, inferences follow. But what is at issue is precisely the premise that life itself is worthwhile; life is the origin of all our knowledge and truth. Nor does "proof" mean empirical certainty based upon verification, for in the range of experience there are no certainties. In a strict sense, that life is worthwhile is not amenable to a descriptive confirmation; it is not capable of being tested as other hypotheses are. Rather, it is a normative postulate, on the basis of which I live.

There is, then, a second question—not the epistemological demand for proof of life's value—but the quest for psychological stimulus and motivational appeal. What is at issue here is whether we can find within life's experience its own reward. Many persons in times of desperation and defeat lose the desire for life, and cry in the darkness for assurance that they ought to continue. Can we provide the sustenance they seek? Surely not, as I have said, by means of any logical or empirical proof. For these persons the will-to-live has its source deep within their psycho-biological nature. If it is absent, what can we say? Does this mean that the value of life is merely irrational preference and quixotic caprice? No—there is more than that. We can give reasons and point to overlooked facts and consequences in seeking to persuade a desperate person not to commit suicide. We can try to arouse an affirmative attitude, hoping that the person will find *some* redeeming features remaining in life, by considering the possibilities: the beauty of dawn and sunset, the pleasures of eating and making love, friends and music and poetry.

Life must have some attractions, and stimulate some interests. But what if it does not? What if the pain and sorrow are too great? For some people life may not be worth living in every context and at any price. In some situations, a sensible person may conclude that death with dignity is the only recourse: an incurable cancer accompanied by great suffering, a burden to the family, a betrayal of incalculable wretchedness, the defeat of a person's most important aims, the death of a loved one, a life of slavery or tyranny—these things may for some be too crushing and overwhelming to endure. The point is, it is not simply biological existence that we seek; modern medicine keeps many people alive. It is the *fullness of life* that we want; if that is completely absent, a heroic exit may be one's only recourse. I may conclude that I would rather die on my feet as a free man, than on my knees as a slave or on my back as an invalid without interest or passion.

The humanist need not answer the theist or existentialist by justifying the view that life is always worth living, that people must be motivated to believe this when they cannot. We can make no universal claim. What we can say is that most human beings, in normal conditions, find life worthwhile. But, I reiterate, it is not simply life at all costs that men seek, but the good life, with significant experience and satisfaction.

It is nonetheless true that for the humanist the cardinal "sin" is death; survival is our highest obligation. Self-defense against injury or death is a necessary precondition; we tend naturally to wish to preserve ourselves. The continuance of life remains an imperative rooted within our basic animal nature. If life seems empty it is usually because our basic needs are unsatisfied and our most important desires frustrated. When misfortune befalls a person and sadness is his companion, he may still respond that though daily life may seem insurmountable, and though one's spirits may appear suffocated by events, still one ought not to give in; one ought to fight to survive.

Why? Again—one cannot "prove" this normative principle to everyone's satisfaction. Living beings tend instinctively to maintain themselves and to reproduce their own kind. This is the primordial fact of life; it is pre-cognitive and pre-rational and it is beyond ultimate justification. It is a brute fact of our contingent natures; and it has its roots within, an instinctive desire to live. The deepest sources of our being yearn for it.

THE FULLNESS OF LIFE

There is, as I have already indicated, another vital normative principle, concomitant with the will-to-live; that is, that we seek, not simply to live, but *to live well*. What we want is a full life in which there is satisfaction, achievement, significance.

What is the good life? What constitutes fullness of being? What is significant satisfaction? Philosophers such as Plato, Aristotle, Spinoza, Bentham, and Mill have reflected upon the nature of the good life, as have prophets, poets, theologians, judges, psychiatrists—experts and plain men alike. Philosophers in the twentieth century generally have cautiously eschewed the question because they have been fearful of committing the so-called "naturalistic fallacy"; that is, in assuming their value judgments as objectively resident in the nature of things—which they are not. Granted the analytic pitfalls, it is still important that we revisit the question, for the nature of the good life is a perennial concern in every culture and every epoch. Even if there is danger that we are merely engaging in "persuasive definitions" of "good" and "bad," it is important that in every period some efforts be made to redefine the excellences of the good life.[1]

[1] See the article by John P. Anton, "Human Excellence," in *Moral Problems in Contemporary Society*, ed. by Paul Kurtz, Englewood Cliffs, N.J., Prentice-Hall, 1969, pp. 116-134.

Even if the moral life is not to be resolved by metaphysics, logic, or science alone, there are degrees of rationality, and our principles can be informed by analysis.

Thus we may ask, what are the characteristics of a life well-lived, at least for contemporary man? As I have said, what most men seek is not simply life or bare existence, but the good life, what philosophers have usually called "happiness." What precisely happiness is, however, is open to dispute. It is not an ideal Platonic quality resident in the essence of man or in the universe at large; it is concrete, empirical, and situational in form and content. It is a concept relative to individuals, their unique needs and interests, and to the cultures in which they function. As such, happiness is in constant need of reformulation. Nor is it elusive or unattainable, as the theist believes; it is fully achievable if the proper conditions are present. Historically, there has been confusion about whether happiness refers to *eudaemonia,* health and well-being, to peace and contentment, or to pleasure and enjoyment. I wish to use the term in a somewhat different way to designate a state or *fullness of being*—a life in which qualities of satisfaction and excellence are present. What, at least in outline, would such a life entail?

Pleasure

The hedonist is correct when he says that a full life should contain enjoyment or excitement. It is difficult to achieve a full life if there is excessive pain or suffering, particularly over long periods of time. To live a full life, one must be able to enjoy a wide range of interests and experiences: delicious food, good drink, sexual love, adventure, achievement, friends, intellectual and aesthetic pleasures, the joys of nature and physical exercise; and one's experiences must be marked by a reasonable degree of tranquility and a minimum of protracted anxiety. It is a mistake, however, to identify pleasure totally with the full life, as hedonists have done. For one may have hedonistic thrills, yet be miserable; one may pursue pleasure and suffer a mundane, narrow existence. The complete sensualist or opium eater may undergo intense pleasurable excitement, but be in a state of melancholy, grief, or boredom. Although moderate amounts of pleasure would appear to be a necessary condition of the good life, pleasure is not a sufficient condition for the fullness of being; the hedonist indeed may be the unhappiest of men.

There are, of course, many varieties of hedonism. There are, for example, voluptuary hedonists, who flit from one sensation to the next in an intense quest for physical pleasures. But the voluptuary can rarely find life satisfying. Did Don Juan, Casanova, or Alcibiades lead full lives? Does the alcoholic, glutton, or addict? The search for new thrills and the focus on the immediate usually mask an under-lying insecurity and instability; they are often signs of immaturity and irresponsibility. Children scream and demand instant gratification; adults learn from experience that it is often wiser to defer gratifica-tion. The voluptuary's appetites for touch and taste constitute a vital aspect of the good life, but surely not the be-all or end-all of human existence.

Recognizing that such a life may lead to anxiety and pain, some hedonists, such as Epicurus, have preached the quiet pleasures, advo-cating retreat from the cares of the world in order to achieve a neutral state of *ataraxia*. They seek peace of soul and emancipation from tension. Quiet hedonism has often meant withdrawal from the ad-venture of life, a limiting of experience, a narrowness rather than a fullness of life. A glass of wine, a piece of cheese, and a quiet gar-den constitute a closed universe. Aesthetic hedonists, such as Walter Pater, have emphasized the cultivation of taste, especially the joys to be gained from works of art. But this model is in the end precious, appropriate for a leisure class rather than for doers. Other hedonists focus on intellectual, spiritual, or religious pleasures. Still others, such as utilitarians, emphasize the moral pleasures of altruistic dedication —pleasures that require development by means of education, and compete with the physical pleasures of food, drink, sex. It is often asked: Which pleasures are "higher" on the scale of values and which are "lower"? Many moralists consider the biological pleasures demeaning, and the aesthetic, intellectual, moral, and spiritual pleas-ures superior.

Hedonists have located an enduring truth about the human condi-tion: Without some pleasure life would not be worth living. But they make a cardinal mistake in isolating pleasure from the process of living. Pleasure is intimately intermingled with life-activity and different kinds of experience; what we seek to attain in a full life is a vigorous mood receptive to varieties of enjoyment, as Lucretius and Goethe recognized. Aristotle observed that pleasure is part and parcel of the good life, helping to complete and bring it to fruition, but that the person who seeks it preeminently will probably never find it. Pleasure must accompany and qualify certain fundamental life activities. Nor are pleasures to be measured quantitatively by any hedonist calculus, as Mill noted, but judged qualitatively. The pleasures of a developed human being have an appeal that infantile hedonists are unable to appreciate.

To come back to our earlier question: Which pleasures ought we to prefer? The basic biological pleasures, or the developed pleasures of an educated and sophisticated being? Efforts by moralists to prove that the so-called "higher" pleasures have a claim and quality intrinsically superior to the "lower" pleasures seem to me to fail. A librarian who can appreciate good books, fine music, and art but not enjoy sex is not necessarily leading a fuller life than the bucolic maiden who cannot read or write but who enjoys the thrills of sexual delight. Granted that the person who knows only physical pleasures but has never cultivated his sensibilities is limited in his range of appreciation. But it is an exaggeration to maintain, as Mill does, that educated people who have tasted both the so-called higher and lower pleasures invariably prefer the former. If it comes to a choice between an orgasm or a sonata, most persons who are honest would seize the former. But it is not really a question of one or the other; in a full life we want both. To ask, which ultimately we should prefer—an embrace or a moral deed, a steak or a symphony, a martini or a poem—is senseless; we want them all.

Satisfaction of Our Basic Needs

To realize the fullness of life requires some satisfaction of basic needs. Without it we are prey to malaise; there are certain norms of health that must be satisfied. The wisest of men have recognized that health is the most precious of possessions, more important than riches or fame. Contingent upon our biological and socio-cultural nature are needs or lacks that we must reduce or satisfy if we are to achieve organic and psychic health. Since I have elsewhere described these needs at length,[1] I will only outline them briefly here.

Our basic needs are of two dimensions: *bio-genic,* that is, they have biological and psychological origins and roots, and *socio-genic,* that is, they are made manifest in and are given content through society and culture.

(a) The primary need of the organism is of course to survive. Threats in the environment must be overcome; injury must be avoided. Natural biological mechanisms of self-protection have evolved, fairly simple in some species but complicated in the human species— an in-built set of structures that operate constantly to preserve the integrity of the organism. Fear of death is the deepest of human forebodings; it is from this primal source, as I have argued, that religions are fed. Fear has roots deep within our somatic nature. It assumes profound psychological and sociological dimensions in civilization. Where the rule of the jungle prevails, any form of peaceful life is impossible. Civilization is possible only because it affords security and protection for individuals. Life need not be dangerous and brief; it may be enjoyable and long, but only if the social environment guarantees this.

(b) A concomitant requirement is the need of the organism to maintain itself and function biologically by achieving homeostasis. The simplest requirements are oxygen, water, food, shelter. As the human ingests materials from his environment in order to survive, the struggle for self-preservation is dependent upon finding that which will make life possible. The organism tends naturally toward a state of equilibrium; any rupture in it stimulates counter-activity to restore the state of organic harmony. There is an organismic tone of the whole body that is essential for well-being. Social institutions come into being to serve basic biological needs; the economic structure of society, methods of production and distribution, make available a range of goods necessary for survival.

(c) Related to these needs are those of growth: egg and sperm, fertilization and fetus, to infant, child, and adult. At different periods of life different needs and capacities emerge. Each stage of life has

[1] Paul Kurtz, *Decision and the Condition of Man,* Seattle, University of Washington Press, 1965.

its dimensions and expectations: exuberance in childhood, impetuosity and idealism in youth, the perspective of maturity and the virtues of wisdom or accomplishment in old age.

(d) Reproduction is essential to the species. Nature rewards those who engage in the act of copulation, necessary for sexual reproduction, by intense pleasure. Our whole being yearns to love and be loved, to hold and be held, to fondle, embrace, penetrate or be penetrated, to be one with another. The celibate faces a void, which he may try to fill but never can. The world is denuded for those who suffer sexual famine, and no degree of sublimation or substitution can make up for it. Although sexuality instinctively serves a reproductive function, it exerts a more powerful claim upon us and plays a vital role in psychosomatic health.

Many philosophers who have written about happiness have overlooked sexual satisfaction. Happiness is not primarily, as the Greeks thought, a matter of cognitive reason; it requires deep-seated emotional satisfaction and psychic adjustment. Freud has made us aware of how we ignore sexuality at our peril. Unhappiness, neurosis, and pathology are bred in sexual frustration and repression.

(e) The need to discharge surplus energy is another organic requirement. We see it more graphically in children and animals, as they romp and play games, but it is also present of course in adults: We need to relax and wind down. Amusement and entertainment, which release us from built-up anxieties and tensions, are expressive experiences that give a special quality to life. Are these only frills? Not simply, for organisms spill out over-abundant reserves; and expressive play is one way by which they do so. Surplus energy is also released by physical exercise and work; we feel vital after exercise, a walk or a swim; it is an expressive need which appears to be related to the tendency to reach levels of homeostasis and equilibrium. Reservoirs of energy need to be released for healthy functioning.

The bio-genic needs apply not only to all forms of human life but to animal life as well.

But man does not live as an isolated individual. The family, tribe, clan—small and large forms of society—help to satisfy our needs and fulfill our interests. Our socio-genic needs help us to realize our biological needs and allow them to develop a primacy of their own, but the mere satisfaction of biological needs is not enough for civilized man. The fullness of life—its variety and quality—is always related to the cultural context in which we exist, and whether or not we flourish depends upon the materials of culture with which we work.

Each of our primary needs is transformed and extended by culture. Food and drink are necessary for survival, but their refinements —infinitely various recipes, subtleties of preparation, cultivation of wines, sophisticated settings, appropriate circumstances—all are social inventions conditioned by our culture; and so our needs are eventually transformed by complexity. The same principle characterizes the relation of sex to society. As a necessity of survival, its nature is transfigured by the considerations of love, by passion, by its significance in the changing mores of marriage and divorce, by its practice in deviant forms, by its exploitation as commerce—all expressive of evolving cultural concepts.

Thus biology and culture converge upon us. Both chance and causality make us what we are. The challenge for each man, though he is culture-bound and time-bound, is to make what he can of his life, to savor his finite moment in history. There are as many models of excellence as there are individuals.

We can never go back; as cultural change moves rapidly, we need always to make and remake what we are, to live authentically while we can. Given all our differences, there are general socio-genic, as there are bio-genic, needs that apply to all men; and there are excellencies that qualify the good life. It is useful to try to spell them out. Though they are no doubt limited by our culture—other cultures and other times may reject them—they are nevertheless pertinent to us and perhaps to most men and cultures.

(f) If literature and art, psychology and religion, and indeed all experience, teach us anything, it is the power of love in human life. There is no doubt about its central importance. No one can live entirely alone, without the affection of others and without being able to reciprocate.

Love has two primordial roots: one, in the dependency of the young, in the mutual need and affection that develops out of the mother's care of the child, and the other in orgasmic sexual arousal and attraction. But there are of course other dimensions and levels, all revealing how dependent we are upon others; and our very self-image is defined by the responses of others to us, as we define theirs. Among the finest and most enduring moments of life are those that we share with others. It is not enough that we receive love or appreciation, we need also to give it. To want only to be loved is infantile, possessive, hardly conducive to growth. To genuinely want the loved one to flower, to be interested in the interests of the other—this is the perfection and reach of human love: in the parent willing to allow his child to become what he will, following his own vision of truth and value; and similarly in the man or woman who, in regard for the loved one, wishes him or her to be a full individual in his or her own sense. Reciprocal love is not necessary for survival, nor even for sexual enjoyment, but its presence is always a sign of a full life. Unless one develops mutual relationships and thus experiences the joys of life, whether with a beloved, a parent, a child, a friend or colleague, one's heart tends to close, one's roots become dry.

(g) Another pre-condition for a good life, and related to love, is the ability to develop a generalized sense of community, to broaden horizons, to belong. Many today are alienated because they have discovered no goals they can share with their fellow humans. In the long history of mankind, the extended family or the tribe, the village or town, have been able to nourish this need. No man who is an island finds life fully significant. During the feudal period each man had his station and his duties, which, though unjust to those at the bottom of the social hierarchy, tended to give a sense of psychological security, some identity. Post-modern man tends to be rootless; he rarely has a beloved community with which he can identify. Unable to participate in common goals, he feels outside.

Belonging to some community has in the past assured interaction on various levels. A small group in which there was face to face encounter was the bedrock of the human relationship. However, as society changes and population increases, as small units coalesce and are absorbed by larger ones, men tend to broaden their sense of community and allegiance. One's community may include his state or nation, religion or culture; eventually it may refer to the brotherhood of man. Religion at its finest has attempted to inculcate a more universal commitment to that moral point of view which treats all men as equal in dignity and value and encourages a deeper concern.

(h) There is an important element in the quest for well-being that religious and philosophical theories have often underestimated—the need for self-affirmation, the need to love one's self. This is as important for our sanity as love of others. I do not speak of those who, puffed up with pride, self-centered, or selfish, need to be restrained for the sake of society, but of those who have too low an estimation of their talent and worth and therefore little self-respect. Indeed, they are often victimized by self-hate, though it is hidden from consciousness, and assumes the different forms of self-deprecation, perfectionism, timorousness, excessive caution, or extreme forms of asceticism. A form of self-pride that is balanced and temperate, as Aristotle noted, is important for our well-being, for a healthy reaction to daily challenges. Every human being has something to contribute, but he cannot do so if he finds little value in his own individuality.

(i) This leads to a vital element: creative actualization. Individuals need more than to satisfy their basic needs; they need bring into fruition their potentialities. This means that there should be a striving to develop. Unless this effort is made, the fullness of life will not be realized. The ideal of creative self-actualization is essential to the concept of happiness that I am delineating. It is actualization of my basic species needs, those that I share in common with other men, but it is individualized; it expresses my unique and personal idiosyncrasies and talents. The injunction is to be myself, not what others would have me be; I must express my own nature in all its variety, and create something new.

This is an activist model of life; it calls upon us to expend energy, to realize what we can be—not what we are; nature is in a process of unfolding. There is no complete, static human essence or nature that defines me and that I merely need to uncover and fulfill. Rather, I am constantly being made and remade in dynamic processes of growth and discovery.

I have certain native capacities but, largely unstructured, they can take various forms. The direction I choose depends upon the cultural context in which I act as well as upon my native abilities. To act is to bring something new into existence. The goal is creativity, the spring of life.

The full life in the last analysis is not one of quiet contentment, but the active display of my powers and of their development and expansion. The creative life involves exploration and curiosity, discovery and ingenuity, the delight in uncovering and introducing novelty. This life is one of forward thrust; the achievement motive dominates. To venture, to experiment—these are the delights of the ongoing spirit, which untap and express hidden powers and implicit capacities, and formulate or create new ones. It is natural to regret a wasted life— a child prodigy who fizzles out, a unique talent that lies fallow, a great person who is reduced by burdens—and to applaud a creative person, whatever his endeavor or area of excellence.

To succeed is not merely to attain one's ends; rather it is to exceed them. The model that I am presenting is contrary to the historically idealized quest for a state of eternal bliss. It proposes enjoyment achieved by full participation in life, not necessarily as defined by society, but as found in an individual's search. Perhaps this exuberant approach is an expression of cultural bias, even of individual pathology. Other civilizations have emphasized the value of meditation and spiritual exercise. Is the incessant quest for achievement simply self-serving ambition? And is this not possibly self-defeating? Do we not in the process often lose the capacity to appreciate the immediacies of experience? Not as I conceive it. This creative model exults in the present moment. It does not necessarily involve a quest for public approval; creative individuals frequently must move against the times. The achievement motive refers to ambition in more personal terms: our wish to excel by our own vision of what life can afford. The spirit of contemplation, like that of celibacy and the priestly mood, if over-emphasized, may express fear, even neurosis, a withdrawal from the challenges of life. I do not deprecate contemplation as part of my nature, a source of intellectual joy and peace. What I am criticizing is the notion that the contemplative life is to be pursued to the exclusion of all else, and that it is the highest form of sainthood. My model of the true "saint" is Promethean man, the creative doer. The counter-culture properly points to the false values of the competitive society. The option we face, however, does not make it necessary to withdraw from the strenuous mood; for we can use it to our own ends.

Audacity, Freedom, and Reason

The ability to live a creative life involves audacity, a defining characteristic of man and a key to his greatness. The audacious life is a life of risk-taking. The nobility of man is not simply that he can develop the courage to be, but to become.

There are the fearful and weak—people of little imagination and daring—who warn that this or that is absolutely unattainable and cannot be done. But the advance of civilization is sparked by the decision not to accept the clichés of one's age, not to be penned in by nature or caged in by history. Man as a Promethean figure is venturesome and bold. These are the virtues of the true heroes and geniuses of history, who have given us new ideas and inventions, new departures in truth and beauty, non-conformists who would not take No for an answer, independent spirits who have made up the roll call of progress.

All human beings have some capacity to be self-activated, provided they are willing to recognize their freedom and seize it, and not to become mired in limitations. I am not by this asserting that determinism is false. We are determined by antecedent conditions, but organic life expresses a form of teleonomic causality. There is no contradiction in affirming that we are both free and conditioned, autonomous and determined. Determinism is not a metaphysical generalization about the universe; it is simply a rule governing scientific inquiry; it presupposes that if we inquire, we will most likely discover the causal conditions under which we act. It need not deny that human life is self-affirming nor that we can create goals and strive to attain them.

The free person is autonomous because he is unwilling to forfeit his existence to external events, but resolves to control them himself. He acts freely insofar as he can, recognizing not only the constraints within a situation, but also the potentialities. Man *is* possibility, an open and dynamic system where alternatives are discovered and created. We are what we will and we can become what we dream. Not all of our dreams can come true—only a madman believes that they can—yet some can, if they are acted upon by reason and experience and applied to the realities of nature.

Though each of us is unique, we are all faced with a similar challenge to create our own future; our lives are the sum of the projects to which we commit ourselves. The term "lifework" is here appropriate. A full life involves artistic vision and creation. The person with a career he enjoys and finds rewarding is the most fortunate of humans, especially if he can blend labor and action, work and play, and can turn his work into a fulfilling outpouring of his self, an expression and an adventure. Our lifework should be measured not only in relation to job or career, for there are many significant sources of creativity: to build one's house, become involved in a cause, act in a play, travel, or become a chef are all forms of enterprise in which a personality can express himself in excellence. The full life is psychologically abundant, bursting at the seams, capable of exulting in consummatory experiences.

This does not mean that life does not have its defeats and failures. Our best laid plans often fail. Our loved ones die. We are aware of the breakdown of means, the tragic conflicts of ends, the abandonment of plans, the moments of despair. Unless these events are completely overwhelming, a rational person can take them in his stride. The creative person is capable of some measure of stoic wisdom.

Human freedom, however, is most complete when our actions are determined by rational means. Can one who is irrational not be happy? Does not happiness basically involve emotional satisfaction? Philosophers have thought that reason was the essential key to the good life. They have no doubt overestimated the rational life and underestimated the deeper forces in our somatic and unconscious behavior. Human beings surely may achieve contentment without developing their full rational faculties; they may lead enjoyable lives and even be capable of some degree of creativity. Yet one who doesn't develop his rational ability is deprived; like the virgin who suffers sexual starvation, such a person is incapable of full functioning. Reason expresses and has become for most humans a crucial bio-social need rooted in our cultural history, necessary if we are to develop fully as individuals.

How and why? In a negative sense, because it is the method of overcoming deception. Human beings, as we have seen, are all too prone to credulousness, to seize upon false idols. Without reflection, we become prey to quackery, whereas reason uses logical analysis and evidence to debunk falsehood and expose fraud. As such, it is an instrument of liberation and emancipation, a source of freedom from illusion.

In a positive sense, rational impulse provides us with both science and ethics. Reflective experience has a double role: in developing an awareness and understanding of the external world and in formulating the values by which we live. In the practical life reason cannot exist independently of our passionate nature. It is the union of thought and feeling that is essential to happiness. Reason that is divorced from its biological roots becomes abstract and oppressive. Cognition that is fused with affection and desire in lived experience expresses the whole person. In the final analysis, it is critical intelligence that best enables us to define and develop our moral principles; and although reason alone is never sufficient for the fullness of life, it is a necessary condition for its attainment.

VI / Moral Libertarianism

Principles

Throughout history, a great number of diverse moral principles have been defended, many of them in opposition to others. Encased in tradition, sanctified by religion and law, moral principles become fixed norms, resistant to change. Accordingly, it is necessary that we reexamine presuppositions, redefine them, and if necessary, reinvest them with new meaning or reconstruct them radically.

We are at a juncture in history where inherited traditions in morality are being questioned or abandoned. What should take their place? If man exists for himself, his morality must serve him; it should not be hostage to religious tradition or metaphysical ideology based upon faith or mystery.

If the first humanist principle is that the full life is worth living, the second is the principle of moral libertarianism, the ideal that all

107

social structures that suppress, denigrate, or alienate the individual should be removed. This is to begin with implicit in the first humanist principle: Social institutions should be judged not by abstract theory, but by how they help the individual to attain the good life.

What is the meaning of freedom or liberty in the moral sense? How far may it be developed? What are the claims of individual freedom? What are the appropriate roles and limits of authority? How relate the individual to society or state? The libertarian would defend personal freedom, broadly conceived; he would seek to emancipate individuals from all forms of arbitrary authority or power that tend to limit free choice. The libertarian principle has been applied, sometimes contradictorily, to a wide range of actions, to thought and belief, taste and appreciation, moral standards and values, political and economic behavior. Inasmuch as man is a socio-cultural animal, living with others in a complex society, it is necessary that his freedom be restricted. But to what degree should he be left alone; what are the appropriate areas of individual choice and action?

Those who defend a conservative point of view claim that social institutions perform a necessary function, that they embody the collective wisdom of the race. According to this view, through long historical processes of trial and error the spurious is discarded and the valuable retained. Reason and order come to prevail. What remains is the best judgment of what is right and good in practice. The inference is that we have a moral obligation to fulfill our social roles. We also have a duty to abide by the laws and customs of the day, to restrain our inclination to flout conventions. Habit and law are supposed to serve the individual and the common good. By submitting to their authority a person realizes his deeper nature and his greater self-interest and freedom. The conservative who so defends the status quo is often more patient with injustice and the forces of coercion and violence used against individuals. But what appears to be rational from the top of the hierarchical order is seen as oppressive by those in less fortunate positions. Indeed, far from holding that it makes both rationality and freedom possible, there are those who condemn the social order for being the main instrument of oppression of the individual.

Various criticisms may be made of the conservative defense of convention. Generally, the opposing view may be said to be libertarian, though there are different kinds of libertarianism. Though traditional labels are deceptive, we can distinguish among "conservative," "liberal," and "radical" kinds of libertarianism. The conservative libertarian is primarily interested in restricting the power of the government, particularly in the economic sphere. The liberal libertarian is interested in maximizing freedom of choice and in providing the conditions that will make individual development possible. The radical, on the other hand, tends toward anarchistic, revolutionary, and socialist ideals, and emphasizes the need for community. Despite their differences, libertarians share a common desire to liberate the individual from authoritarian institutions.

Most, though not all, libertarians have a positive view of human nature. They believe that men are basically good, noble, capable of mutual aid and cooperation, and wish to help their fellow creatures. Some libertarians view human nature in non-social dimensions. One influential theory claims that the individual enters into a social contract with the state wherein he agrees to relinquish part of his liberty on the condition that it protect him. But, they say, the compact has been unfortunate, since the state has emerged as a super-Goliath, all-powerful, tyrannical, and far more corrupt than the original state of nature. Hence, they consider it necessary to limit or destroy the state, and restore the individual to his earlier conditions of liberty and peace. Some libertarians, drawing on Hobbes, hold an atomistic view of man as an isolated being, self-interested and self-seeking, who enters into a social contract for convenience. Other libertarians, drawing on Locke and Rousseau, also assume the view that the individual is atomistic and that he creates the state artificially, but they view man as a noble animal with social sentiments, and they wish to provide the conditions whereby he can express his nature.

ANARCHISM

There are other libertarians, however, who entirely reject individualistic premises. Man, according to them, is thoroughly social; hence any pre-social or idealized account of the individual is a distortion. This form of libertarianism is anarchistic. Since anarchism is enjoying great popularity today, it is useful to examine it in some detail.

Maximoff Bakunin and Peter Kropotkin are the two leading proponents of anarchism. They believe in the intrinsic moral characteristics of man. Kropotkin claims that there is a deep community spirit in man, a tendency not for competition of all against all, as Hobbes or Darwin said, but for mutual aid and assistance. He maintains that "the mutual aid tendency in man . . . is so deeply interwoven with all the past evolution of the human race, that it has been maintained by mankind up to the present time, notwithstanding all vicissitudes of history." Indeed, he considers all new, progressive ethical systems, religious, economic and social institutions to be simply an extension of the mutual aid principle. This principle allows for "great latitude for individual initiative," responding at the same time to man's need of mutual support.[1]

Similarly, Bakunin says that "emerging from the condition of the gorilla, man arrives only with difficulty at awareness of his humanity and realization of his liberty." He comes into the world as a ferocious being, he is progressively humanized and emancipated only in the midst of society. "Man realizes his individual freedom only by rounding out his personality with the aid of other individuals belonging to the same social environment."[2]

The individual does not exist in a pre-social state of liberty and bliss; rather, society is the fountain and source of his appreciation of liberty and of his humanity. Man does not create society, says Bakunin, out of an artificial social compact; he is born into it. He is not born free, but in fetters, as a result of the social environment in which he exists.

Both Kropotkin and Bakunin consider the state to be the main repressive institution; Bakunin especially condemns private property and the class structure as a form of social oppression. Thus, revolutionary and socialist anarchists wish to destroy the state, with

---

[1] Peter Kropotkin, *Mutual Aid, A Factor of Evolution*, (1914 edition), Boston, Extending Horizons Books, Porter Sargent (pp. 223-224).
[2] *The Political Philosophy of Bakunin: Scientific Anarchism*, ed. by G. P. Maximoff, Glencoe, The Free Press, 1953, p. 237.

its apparatus of police, law, and bureaucracy; they want to seize the forces of production and transform them by means of collective ownership. Bakunin was especially critical of Marx, Engels, and the German communists for wanting to establish a "dictatorship of the proletariat" during the transitional period to communism. He was prophetic: in destroying the capitalist hold on the machinery of state power, the proletariat, in seizing political power, would merely replace one form of oppression by a minority with another. The abolition of both state and church, he said, must be the first, indispensable condition of the real enfranchisement of society. Bakunin believed in the use of violence to destroy or liquidate the state entirely. In this sense, he distinguished libertarian revolutionists, who were partisans of the absolute destruction of the state, from authoritarian communists, who were not. In opposition to anarchism, Marx waged a bitter tirade against Bakunin and succeeded in wresting control of the International Workingman's Association from him.

Kropotkin too was critical of the use of state power. After years of exile, he returned to Russia after the Revolution of 1917; indeed, he was offered a post in the government by Kerensky, which he declined. Deeply shocked by Lenin's and the Bolsheviks' use of state power, he wrote in 1920 to Lenin deploring the Bolshevik practice of taking hostages to protect themselves against possible violence from their opponents. He asked, "What future lies in store for communism when one of its most important defenders tramples in this way on every honest feeling?"[3]

Anarchists are thus opposed to political and governmental power; they consider the state to be a relatively recent development in human evolution; and they wish to destroy it and return man to the virtues of communal life and mutual aid.

The state is surely not an eternal institution. In my judgment, man should, on one hand, attempt to transcend it by developing small-scale decentralized units. On the other hand, we need to bring into being a supernational law and government endowed with authority greater than that of separate national governments. There have been an incredible number of crimes committed by national states; in the

[3] From "Foreword" by Ashley Montagu, *Mutual Aid, A Factor of Evolution, op. cit.*

most extreme form, wars in which countless millions have undergone untold suffering and lost their lives. The state has fostered totalitarian systems in which individuals are controlled by police networks of terror and imprisonment. Though patriotism may be considered to be a noble virtue within a national state and against foreign oppression, it is antihumanistic, setting people against people. It has led, not to peace and cooperation, but to economic rivalries and exploitation on a world-wide scale. National states now control means of terrible destruction, and this situation is exacerbated because they are laws unto themselves, but they are certainly not the only institutions that have developed excessive power; economic, religious, and other institutions have done the same. National states have undoubtedly had important positive roles. They have provided a basis for common cultural values, a language stock, culinary arts, a rich artistic heritage; they have secured within their borders some measure of political order and economic well-being, and enabled people to live and work together under conditions of relative harmony. They have promulgated systems that have made civilized life possible.

Obviously the libertarian or anarchist who thinks that all political or governmental regulations can be dispensed with is being deceived by utopianism. Given the complexities of modern life, some procedure for regulating public behavior is essential. Without a system of humane law and just order, life would be impossible.

A utilitarian justification of political order and social regulation hence appears to be necessary. The issue is not whether there should be regulation, but how much and in what sphere. No absolute principles apply here. Nevertheless, I would maintain that the state at least ought not intervene in matters concerning private morality and values, and that, if it does intervene, its intervention should be minimal. We ought as individuals to have some autonomy concerning our beliefs, tastes, values, our deepest goals, unless an urgent question of the social good is at stake.

LIBERTARIANISM IN THE MORAL SPHERE

There are libertarians who take their analysis deeper, who consider not only the state, but other social institutions, perhaps all, to be repressive. Some liberal and conservative libertarians reject a socialist program believing that the collective organization is liable to destroy the free choice of the individual; and they wish to defend the uniqueness of individuality against all pressures. They are as opposed to communal anarchism as to the state.

John Stuart Mill in *On Liberty* provides the most thoroughgoing defense of libertarianism. For him, it is both the state and society that need to be restructured, though neither can ideally "wither away." Society in general ought to allow individuals to pursue their own lives, satisfy their tastes, fulfill their destinies, and discover whatever unique truths and values they can, so long as they do not interfere with the rights of others to do likewise. The famous passage from Mill reads:

> The sole end for which mankind are warranted, individually or collectively, in interfering with the liberty of action of any of their number is self-protection. That the only purpose for which power can be rightfully exercised over any member of a civilized community, against his will, is to prevent harm to others.[4]

Does Mill's principle provide a criterion for the appropriate domain of individual liberty and enable us to determine when the state or society may intervene? Mill emphasized the need for negative limits, although he did not spell out what he meant by "harm." But his principle lacks due regard for the positive reaches of social policy and for the social good. He recognized this, however, in his later writings, when he was more sympathetic to socialist considerations.

There are many forms of individual freedom and many kinds of regulations of conduct. Leaving aside the question of political and economic liberty for the moment, the central question that I wish to focus upon is: to what degree should an individual be given latitude in his private life to pursue the good life as he sees it? What is the domain of his unique and idiosyncratic concern? What is at issue here is the nature and extent of moral freedom that society ought to suffer or tolerate in its citizens.

[4] John Stuart Mill, *On Liberty* in *Utilitarianism, Liberty and Representative Government,* New York, Dutton, 1950, p. 73.

Sexual Morality

It is regrettable that political and social authorities have so often sought to dictate public policy about matters that should be considered essentially private. Taboos and legal restrictions on sexual activity provide the most flagrant examples of such policy. Why should the state proscribe birth control, abortion, adultery, homosexuality, sodomy, prostitution, divorce? Why should social pressures discriminate against one form of conduct and support others?

The Wolfenden Committee Report in Great Britain recommended useful guidelines: Where sexual relations are between consenting adults, the state ought not to interpose itself. Where a sexual act involves a minor, or is compulsory, as in rape, then the state may intervene to protect the helpless. There have been so many varieties of sexuality practiced in our own and other cultures that it is arbitrary for the state to declare some forms legitimate and others illegitimate.

For the moral libertarian, laws that attempt to prohibit "deviant sexuality" end up by imposing a specialized moral position upon the greater community. Those who because of religious scruples are offended by abortion or birth control are not compelled to engage in either; but in a pluralistic society those who wish to limit their offspring should be permitted to do so without censorship or punishment by the state. If one believes in certain natural or divine laws, one may object to artificial intervention in the sexual process; if one does not begin with that premise, however, sexual activity does not exist only to reproduce, but also for psychic satisfaction and enjoyment; and it may be guided and controlled by natural means. The Roman Catholic Church considers the fetus to be a living "human being"; but the fetus lacks the developed personality or self-consciousness, which defines what it means to be "human." And in the name of its metaphysical-theological doctrine the Church has condoned a repressive policy. It has been insensitive to the suffering and anxiety caused by inflicting unwanted children upon overburdened parents. The refusal even to permit the abortion of those fetuses conceived in rape, those born to minors without their consent, those that are malformed or the product of incestuous relationships, illustrates the intransigence of a dogmatic doctrine. Those who are inflexibly opposed to all abortions are impervious to the deeper nuances of the moral life.

By the same token I do not believe that the woman in all cases should alone decide whether to have an abortion. Though one may convincingly argue that a woman should have control over her own body the male is of course also responsible for the pregnancy. Accordingly, one may argue that whether an abortion should be performed should be determined by both parents whenever possible. Sexuality, where two or more parties are involved, should result from voluntary consent, and the decision concerning a prospective abortion should therefore also be based upon mutual consent, morally, if not legally. Granted that it is the woman who should make the final decision; if she decides to have an abortion, the state should respect her wishes; the decision on moral grounds should, however, be a cooperative one.

The key consideration that should apply to all forms of sexual activity—whether adultery, sodomy, bisexuality, homosexuality, lesbianism—is that the parties are adult and that they freely agree without coercion. Neither the state nor society should seek to define what is permissible or forbidden sexual conduct. Various forms of sexuality have been condemned on medical and moral grounds as "deviant." Yet in recent years the question has been raised whether they are "abnormal." There are those who maintain that such sexuality is fairly widespread and is found in other species as well. Accordingly, it may even be considered a "normal" outlet under certain social and psychological conditions. Should the state or society a priori condemn it and seek to outlaw it? Repressive laws often cause suffering, frustration, fear, self-hate. There are strong arguments for a reduction or abolition of state interference in affairs that are private. For the state to adopt a policy of neglect, however, does not mean that it should condone pandering or ignore the possible danger to impressionable young people. It simply allows consenting adults freedom to express their proclivities without interference.

If this principle should prevail in regard to private behavior, it should not necessarily apply to all forms of public behavior. One should not seek to stamp out prostitution or make it a crime, but one may without contradiction regulate public solicitation that offends others. Thus the state may insist that prostitutes not become a public nuisance. They should be allowed to engage in their profession, if they wish, so long as they do not force their attentions on those who do not wish to be molested. For the rights of those solicited, including those who have compunctions against prostitution, ought to be considered on the same level as those of the prostitute.

On the same basis I do not believe that the state ought to regulate the conditions of marriage or the grounds for divorce, at least for adults. The state ought not to consider traditional monogamy as sacrosanct; there are alternative forms of marriage which may be viable for some—including open marriages, even bigamy, polygamy, homosexual relationships, and group marriages. Whether two (or more) people decide to marry is their own decision and if any party chooses to break the marriage that, too, should be a private affair. The state ought not to make divorce so difficult that it is almost impossible. Present-day divorce laws impose a heavy burden, leading people to fraud or deceit. This often results in intolerable alimony awards to one party in order to secure consent from the other. The most humane approach to the dissolution of a marriage would be the principle of no fault, that is, where a marriage has been irretrievably broken and is no longer viable, individuals ought to be allowed by consent, or by notice to either party, to declare it at an end. The state ought simply to record the fact, not determine its morality or legality. Moreover, awards of lifetime alimony in many cases are barbaric, except where the woman or man is unable to work because of illness or old age. Alimony creates a class of dependents who not only have relinquished autonomy as persons, but are an unfair burden to one who wants to establish or maintain another family.

To say that divorce proceedings and alimony arrangements should be private, however, is to say that it is a matter for adults. It does not and should not apply in the same way when children are involved; society has a responsibility to ensure the welfare of minors, and to see to it that adequate provision is made for their support, care, and education. Indeed, we can argue that the state ought to appoint a public advocate to look after the rights of the innocent, who perhaps suffer most in the lengthy litigation and acrimony that often accompany separation.

Although I have thus far defended a libertarian position concerning the private sexual behavior of individuals, there is one area of sexuality in which I think that the absolute freedom of individuals may need to be controlled. I refer to reproduction and to the vast problem of population increase. Mankind may be reaching a dangerous point at which the strain of random population growth on world resources will lead to catastrophe. If individuals will not restrict the family to two offspring, the state may have to intervene. There are various ways of limiting excessive growth. One method is by means of negative-income-tax incentives, those with more children to be penalized by higher taxes. Concomitant with this is the need for extensive programs of voluntary sterilization. Public education in birth control and abortion needs to be encouraged. However, the situation may reach an explosive stage and more stringent measures may have to be introduced. Procreation, like health, welfare, and defense, may have to become a matter of public policy. The rationale is that with population unchecked, the result may be an undermining of the liberty of all who would have to compete for limited resources and privacy. It is because of our desire to preserve long-range individual freedom that the state may have to intervene.

Similarly, we should not necessarily be averse to the emerging possibilities of bio-genetic engineering. It is not simply the quantity but the quality of population that we should be concerned with. We are rapidly approaching the time when we will be able to program out genetic defects. I surely would not wish to make eugenic control mandatory; I would prefer to use moral persuasion and education. Genetic counseling may afford great potentialities for freedom, for parents of future generations to create individuals endowed with the highest potentialities.

Scientific Engineering and Freedom

This raises the question of the uses of science and whether scientific controls in the future will not mean an end to individual liberty. B. F. Skinner in *Beyond Freedom and Dignity*[5] and *Walden Two*[6] believes there is a need to develop a technology of control, which

[5] N. Y., Knopf, 1971.
[6] N. Y., Macmillan, 1948.

will require abandoning some of our so-called archaic notions of individual "freedom" and "dignity." Those who believe in libertarianism and would allow the maximum individual freedom consonant with the social good are especially disturbed about what appears to be implicit in Skinner's analysis. Skinner holds that genuine individual freedom is an illusion: Since we are conditioned by our environment, he argues, why not recognize this, and use operant conditioning to turn behavior in the directions that we want?

Certain philosophical puzzles emerge from Skinner's thesis. If everything we do is strictly determined, can we choose to control the environment or to follow Skinner's recommendations, unless we are pre-determined to do so? If, on the other hand, we can influence or modify our environmental conditions, do we not have some measure of freedom? "Soft determinism," which holds the latter position, is perfectly compatible with both scientific behaviorism and freedom of choice. It believes that human behavior can be explained by reference to natural causes *and* that we freely select goals and that our choices have consequences in future conduct. Skinner at times appears to be following hard, rather than soft, determinism. His rejection of individual freedom mistakenly follows from this premise. But behavioral science need not presuppose hard determinism nor need it reject freedom; nor, conversely, does libertarianism presuppose a doctrine of metaphysical freedom.

The possible misuses of behavioral technology are a cause for concern to libertarianism. Skinner is no doubt correct when he observes that "To refuse to control is to leave control not to the person himself, but to other parts of the social and nonsocial environment."[7] Thus we should not flee in romantic revulsion from a constructive technology of behavior, but rather use it for the benefit of mankind. The questions are not whether we should utilize the tools of control, but, as Skinner recognizes, who shall do the controlling; for what ends; how shall we control the controllers; should not limits be placed upon such controls? Here I should insist that an uncompromising commitment to a democratic social ethic must be maintained as a safeguard against the Dr. Strangeloves of the future. Claims of

---

[7] *Beyond Freedom and Dignity*, p. 84.

individual freedom and dignity, says Skinner, should not be allowed to stand in the way of necessary social policies and controls.

But the ideals of freedom and dignity should not be so readily dismissed. It is essential in any polity that we place some restraints on those who would exert power over other human beings. Democratic methods of social change may be less efficient, but they entail fewer risks than does centralized technocratic planning. History dramatizes all too well that no group of men, not even of scientific experts, is infallible; there must be some means for influencing and reversing the policies of leaders. Skinner's *Walden Two* is opposed to libertarianism. It also fails to allow for sufficient democratic processes in arriving at basic decisions. Planners must not be permitted to be immune to the ethics of freedom or of democratic control; there is always the danger that they will identify their self-interest with the good of society.

If we are to condition and educate—as all societies do—this effort should be piecemeal and limited, and always open to criticism and modification. It should apply to children, not adults. We should not abandon the ideals of individual dignity and freedom. In behavioral terms, this means that individuals should have the right to challenge those who would use them without their consent.

Granted that we shall continue to teach our children and condition them to become the kinds of human beings that we want. But we also want them to develop independence of judgment and to learn to use their intelligence in framing beliefs and values. As individuals they should share in the power and responsibility of society, the direction and control of the environment and of their private lives. Again a basic question is: How is the power of science to be used and by whom? Libertarianism must not be bartered away by technology.

Drugs and Narcotics

Another question of freedom often troubles many people: Should drugs and narcotics be legalized? If various substances are demonstrably noxious should society undertake to prevent their use? The state, as I have argued, ought not to impose moral restrictions on individuals. The libertarian is reluctant to affect the consumer's right to purchase alcohol, tobacco, or high cholesterol products, even though they are damaging to health. This does not mean, however, that the state should not engage in extensive educational campaigns pointing out their dangers.

In any case, laws should not outstrip public acceptance—as was demonstrated by the failure of prohibition against liquor. This is especially true when the law involves more harmful consequences than the practice it was designed to extirpate, as in the case of prohibition, which led to bootlegging and racketeering. Should other drugs continue to be prohibited? Clearly the penalties against the use of marijuana are outdated and vindictive; they should be reduced, particularly if marijuana is no more harmful to health than whiskey or cigarettes—perhaps still an open question. Heroin is clearly noxious; we deplore its serious misuses. On the other hand, a policy of legal extirpation may be counter-productive and lead to an increase of crime. Though heroin and other narcotics should be heavily taxed and regulated, it may very well be that they should be legalized, at least on the basis of medical prescription, as in the maintenance programs in Great Britain.

No policy provides easy solution. Moral principles are not absolute. One often has to select the lesser evil. One may be committed to libertarianism and yet make exceptions. The decision must always be guided by considering the long-range consequences. In my view, the principle of libertarianism should only be overridden when disastrous results from inaction might affect individual liberty and the social good—as in, for example, a population explosion, a plague, or a major danger to public safety and health—and which may therefore force us, reluctantly and temporarily, to suspend civil liberties. As we have already indicated, moral principles often conflict. Resolution naturally depends upon situation. The state may prevent individuals from littering the streets with garbage, it can demand that pets be inoculated against rabies, or that people do not pollute the atmosphere with incinerators. Libertarianism may be limited when one person's actions prevent others from exercising their rights.

A correlative humanistic principle is that of equal rights; the state or society must not only protect me from harm by others, but must ensure that I have equality of opportunity and that conditions are present for me to fulfill my potentialities. When there is a clash between these two principles—libertarianism and equal rights—priority can be determined only by the context, the observable facts and the consequences of alternatives.

In regard to addictive drugs, a restrictive policy might be defended if it could be shown that there is a clear and present danger to the health and welfare of the community. Like Mill, I would mitigate this with leniency toward users, but severity toward sellers or traffickers, on the principle that my moral life is my own (especially if I am an adult). I do not have an unlimited right to peddle what I want, where I want, when I want. Hence, the state can clearly regulate action related to trade.

Involuntary Commitment

Also of concern to the defender of individual liberty is the increasing tendency to label certain kinds of behavior under the rubric "mental illness." We are all too prone to condemn atypical behavior as "disturbed," "abnormal," "pathological," or "insane," and to commit to mental hospitals individuals who deviate from societal norms. We are well aware that in the Soviet Union political dissidents have been incarcerated in mental institutions. Something similar—though on a less contrived scale, and surely not as part of state policy—occurs when we allow psychiatrists to commit individuals to mental institutions. Some people are unable to function and need hospitalization, but we ought to be sensitive to the dangers of medical diagnoses that only mask the moral prejudices of society and misleadingly impose standards in the name of medicine rather than politics, religion, or morality. The special danger is commitment without the person's consent. The patient's relatives and psychiatrists are permitted tremendous power to circumvent individual freedom.

Serious restrictions also emanate from other institutions of society. Besides repealing laws that regulate moral conduct, beliefs, and values, we ought to minimize the conformist tendencies of public opinion. Institutions such as the church, the corporation, the school, various ethnic groups, limit individual autonomy by imposing all sorts of sanctions, from excommunication to ostracism and economic retaliation, subtle forces which may be more oppressive to the individual than the state is.

Economic Freedom

Does libertarianism imply an individual's right to absolute economic freedom? No. Private property is not sacred, nor is it beyond public control. An individual's right to self-development does not carry with it a right to use private property independently of its impact on others or without any kind of social regulation.

Historically, the problem of economic freedom has been discussed as an issue of free-enterprise capitalism versus socialism or some other type of control; it has been concerned with the entrepreneur's freedom to engage in commerce without undue governmental interference. This is no longer the decisive issue. The reality of the contemporary marketplace is that large-scale corporate organizations have by and large replaced individual decision-makers. In considering the relationship between corporations, labor unions, and other large interest groups that seek to make decisions, we may find in these new conditions an increased need for regulation by planning bodies, particularly by the state, concerned with the effects of economic activity on the well-being of society.

The role of the individual worker or manager within the corporation is often overlooked by the conservative libertarian, so worried about big government that he forgets about repression by private industry. And it is often overlooked by the radical anarchist, who has the illusion that if he merely destroys the state and socializes the means of production, the problem of freedom and alienation would be resolved.

Modern technology has presented the individual with an enormous range of possibilities. It has freed large numbers from drudgery in their labor. Man is no longer condemned to follow the Biblical injunction "In the sweat of thy face shalt thou eat bread." Modern industrial society has reduced the working day and improved economic conditions to such a degree that there is within the grasp of most men the possibility of banishing freedom from want. As a result of the trend toward mass production, many people can now satisfy their basic bio-social needs (including the need for education and culture). Though there are still large areas of poverty and unemployment, such problems are gradually being solved, at least in advanced technological societies. Yet in those societies where the defeat of deprivation is within reach, other forces, more subtle forms of repression, have intervened to limit man's newly won freedom.

The fact is that a sense of alienation is the constant companion of post-modern man, who lives in a depersonalized and dehumanized world. Urbanized, technological society has uprooted him from a rural environment and thrust him into a world of machines, automobiles, air conditioners, skyscrapers, computers, and supersonic travel. In capitalist societies, the individual is measured by his role as a consumer, his needs and values manipulated by those who want his time, money, or vote.

Although drudgery is being minimized by new labor-saving devices, the conditions of labor still have not altered the lifeless character of much work, or the consequent boredom for individuals locked within large economic units. Able to see only a small part of the total operation, they often feel impotent in designing, adding to, or altering the final product of their industry. The price that we have had to pay for mass production has been the virtual end of devoted craftsmanship and creative intensity. Skilled shoemakers and carpenters, even electricians and plumbers, are rapidly disappearing. For increasingly large numbers of people work is merely a means to buying leisure time. There is a divorce of labor from end, process from product. The purposes of the worker's labor are developed by others; he is merely part of a system of production and distribution. Those who are often exempt from such alienating conditions are the managers and the professionals, free to work in creative endeavors, for whom love of work and pride in workmanship, a fusion of means and ends, are still possible. How to liberate the workingman, however, from the complex organization of production is a problem that the technological society has not yet solved.

The same conditions are present in socialist societies, except that the worker does the bidding of the bureaucrat rather than that of the capitalist. The distinction notwithstanding, a steel worker in Detroit or Dansk faces similar problems in relating to the conditions of his labor as does an orderly in a hospital in Canton or Marseilles. The emergence of a managerial class to direct production compounds the problem. Those who control the instruments of production, whether by ownership under capitalism or political power under communism, are responsible for the individual's destiny. This is a basis for new class antagonisms and bureaucratic friction. Marxism has not re-solved the problem of the alienation of labor or the existence of elites.

Overall direction is an essential component of all industrial na-tions, whether the plans emanate from a centralized source in socialist societies or from multi-centralized sources in capitalist and semi-socialist societies, whether large firms, monopolistic or oligopolistic industries, or governments make the decisions. But, we must ask, what is the role of the individual in the process of production? How can he affect the kind of labor expended and the kinds of products produced? One solution is participatory democracy, in which indi-viduals can share in planning the kind of society they want and in helping to forge the decisions of the organizations of which they are a part. This means a trend toward the development of small groups and decentralized efforts, wherever possible.

There are several other hopeful solutions, which I shall mention briefly now and return to in Chapter VIII.

With increased automation, it will be possible to reduce the work week and to effect a vast increase of leisure time for the enjoyment of the arts of life. A work week in some industries is already 35 hours, or four days, leaving much of what was formerly working time for the workers to pursue their private interests. There is no reason why industrial workers eventually will not be able to work a maximum of 30—even 20—hours per week. In order for this to be achieved, how-ever, it is important that life not be compartmentalized into work and play; to consider time spent at work as necessary drudgery, and free time as simply for pleasure, is to disrupt and disorganize life. Indeed, the reverse is often true. People may not be able to tolerate their jobs, but leisure often leads to boredom and anxiety, especially where television is the chief diversion. Even with increased leisure, it is important that work be significant. In addition, by reducing the work week, with work then being shared by more people, it is possible to alleviate the problem of unemployment. We are faced with a ques-tion of value. Do we want more income or more free time? Perhaps we need to develop an appreciation of the arts of creative leisure rather than the gluttony of passive consumption.

Though an overemphasis on work for its own sake may mean the deadening of experience, it is important, with leisure time expanding, that the work ethic not be abandoned. Interest in and capacity for productive work is essential if society is to develop a viable system for freeing people from drudgery, and if the individual is to discover the values of culture in his personal life. We know that many people in industrial organizations and offices waste time by plodding and dreaming from one coffee break to the next. If they worked at full steam, perhaps the problem of "working hours" could be solved. It might even be possible to get rid of the fixed time clock and have people come and go, provided they were motivated to put forth effort; work might even continue at home. Leisure time can be filled with other work projects in a fusion of creative endeavor with leisure and expressive enjoyment. Yet many people are locked into a rigid life of work from eight to five, day in, day out, year after year, with only a few weeks off for vacation. Why not sabbatical leaves for individuals to pursue professional or private interests or further education? Why should we consider higher education as suitable only for the young? Why not college careers later in life, with ample free time to pursue them? We should also favor changing careers in midstream; with many occupations obsolescent, new skills for the performance of new and more meaningful jobs should be widely encouraged.

Because in affluent societies an increasingly larger percentage of the work force is occupied with providing services rather than goods, we have a real opportunity to develop a vital sense of workmanship. We need to encourage young people to become expert craftsmen, independent artisans, capable of serving both their own society's interests simultaneously so that each problem may become a challenge and an adventure for independent effort and creative solution.

We have reached a point where economic growth for its own sake must be questioned. One of the greatest failures of a capitalist society is that without an increased tempo of production the rate of profit may decline and a stagnant economy be followed by recession. What social purpose is there in clogging roadways with millions of automobiles? Why program built-in obsolescence and planned waste by introducing spuriously new models when the so-called old ones are capable of serving? These questions apply both to socialist and capitalist societies, since they have the same drive for growth. Can we limit the excessive emphasis on economic growth? Is it not wiser to replace it by an emphasis on individual and cultural development? If so, the plight of workers may be ameliorated and more of their efforts become involved in cultivation of the arts of life.

TOLERANCE

A principle that underlies much of my discussion thus far—and is essential to the kind of open pluralistic society I have been supporting—is toleration. We ought to respect the rights of others to express beliefs, attitudes, values, and life-styles different from our own.

This principle is increasingly crucial in a society becoming liberated from economic strictures, where the availability of education and leisure will permit an extraordinary variety of possibilities for personal fulfillment. It is also necessary if we are to avoid anti-libertarian applications of our ever-expanding technology.

The principle of tolerance does not imply approval of all individuals or groups; nor does it preclude criticism of them or attempts to persuade them to modify their beliefs, values, or conduct. It says only that we should not suppress or deny them, that people ought to be free to pursue their interests as they see fit, and that we ought to respect their right to do so. I do not wish to argue that we ought to tolerate every kind of action. I am surely not advocating the abolition of all regulation or laws, as the anarchist wants, only those that unduly repress the individual. Every society has some need to regulate conduct and to define permissible action by its laws.

The liberal tradition has clearly enunciated the principle of tolerance, especially as it applies to beliefs and values. In *A Letter Concerning Toleration,* Locke attempted to convince Christians to become more tolerant of other Christians, and opposed the claims of a well-intentioned government to compel "true religion" by force or to establish one sect as true in opposition to others. Similarly, Mill in *On Liberty* provided a masterful defense of freedom of belief and moral conviction.

Toleration is *prima facie* a fundamental normative principle that we ought not to suspend except possibly in extreme circumstances, where a clear and imminent danger from *actions* is involved. This principle is directly relevant to the present socio-historical situations and to various kinds of societies that now exist—capitalist, socialist, communist, feudal, or semi-feudal. We ought to work for the extension of civil liberties and for their defense against those who would limit or deny them. The cause of tolerance is the cause of human progress. In a revolutionary situation, where the goal is a socialist or communist society, it is vital that toleration be maintained during the transitional period. Not to do so risks its total abandonment. If intolerance is a way of life there is danger that the "new man" or "new society" will be intolerant, narrow, and self-righteous.

The following three arguments to justify the principle of tolerance are based upon consideration of the social good.

The first argument is epistemological: To be intolerant of other points of view or systems of value implies, as Mill observed, that you or your group have the absolute truth, or that your philosophy has reached its final, ultimate, most perfect formulation. Charles Peirce pointed out that most claims to infallibility in the history of thought have been falsified, and each effort to define by authority a fixed position, whether ecclesiastical, political, or ideological, has been overturned by some new discovery or hypothesis. No individual or group can claim a monopoly of truth or virtue. We must not block the path to inquiry or research. Let us always leave open the possibility that we may be mistaken and that there may be other points of view that share in meaning and truth. In any case, social problems are so complex that to solve them we need the highest degree of creativity and imagination, coming from all levels of society. Any society that does not allow adventure in thought and invention will stagnate.

The second argument is psychological: Beliefs that are left unchallenged degenerate into dogma, ossified prejudice. Toleration of opposing critical viewpoints allows for the modification of those beliefs that are false and for the strengthening of those that are true. Testing one's beliefs by contest with contrary opinion enables one to transform blind allegiance based upon fear into genuine commitment based upon intelligent participation in the decision-making process.

The third argument for toleration is political: No ruling group or class is all-wise. For those in power to consider their point of view, especially if left unquestioned, to be true is to confuse self-interest with the common good. Societies that tolerate criticism and dissent will of course suffer less from hypocrisy and duplicity than those that are closed.

When I am receptive to other points of view I make it possible not only for myself but also for others to grow and prosper, each in his own way. In being considerate of alternatives, I am able to share in other kinds of experience, other conceptions of truth, beauty, and goodness, and thus expand my horizons and enrich my experience.

If the above arguments have any merit, tolerance is not a mere luxury to be dispensed with or permitted only under certain conditions, but an essential ingredient of any humane society, not grudgingly extended to those for whom we have little use, but recognized as a positive expression of a human ideal.

Yet the principle of toleration has come under attack throughout history—from Plato and the medieval Church to Stalin and Mao. The past has been full of attempts to censor opinions considered false or harmful, to prohibit heresy, to condemn unorthodoxy.

A modern criticism of tolerance deserves special comment. Herbert Marcuse and others in the book *A Critique of Pure Tolerance*[8] attack the principle of pure tolerance, questioning its moral basis and its political and social effect. And in *An Essay on Liberation*[9] Marcuse again raises serious criticisms of the toleration of civil liberties in the so-called bourgeois societies, arguing that in some cases it is permissible to withdraw toleration of others. Capitalist consumer economies, he believes, often fraudulently parade civil liberties which are really forms of "repressive tolerance," used by the power structure to mask its self-interest and to prevent social change. Presumably for Marcuse the left may be intolerant of those tendencies on the right that it finds reprehensible.

Many of his observations about capitalist societies are astute. So-called free capitalist economies permit advertisers to manipulate values and to inculcate wants that are not genuine. In satisfying such values, they develop in consumers a dependence upon the very economic system that seeks to repress them. We should not defend unlimited freedom for advertisers to do whatever they wish without

[8] Robert Paul Wolff, Barrington Moore, Jr., and Herbert Marcuse, eds., Boston, Beacon Press, 1965.
[9] Boston, Beacon Press, 1969.

regard to the social good, but we should defend virtually unlimited intellectual and moral freedoms. It is possible to defend pure tolerance not simply on the usual libertarian grounds with an individualistic theory of human nature, but rather in terms of a social conception of man. One argument against Marcuse's thesis is in the serious blunder that results from the undermining of civil liberties. In many Western countries the left is in a position of basic weakness. It hardly makes sense to advocate intolerance of the "intolerable" when the right finds the views of the left "intolerable" and is all too prepared to suppress them. The great need in socialist countries is to extend toleration to different points of view, not to limit them further.

A familiar pragmatic objection to tolerance, often heard from groups in power, is that it cannot be permitted or given legal sanction because of the danger of revolution. In repressive capitalist societies the most common argument is that censorship and control must operate because to sanction civil liberties is to court subversion. In repressive socialist societies there is a similar argument, namely, that toleration will lead to counter-revolution. But belief must be distinguished from action—a society should tolerate beliefs though it may not wish to permit certain forms of action. In the same way, heresy must be distinguished from conspiracy. If a heretic expresses a point of view in opposition to official policy, or disagrees with prevailing opinion, he is not therefore a conspirator, plotting the violent overthrow of the regime. If a government opposes conspiracy, it should nevertheless appreciate the necessity for the spirit of critical inquiry, permit heresy, and tolerate opposing points of view.

Another objection to toleration is that it has meaning only in relation to certain historical traditions, and hence is not possible where the people are unaccustomed to it. There are societies where toleration is deeply embedded in the national character and has historical precedents (for example, Great Britain); and others intolerant of diversity, whose leaders are extremely sensitive to any criticisms made of them (such as the Soviet Union). Thus, in some societies it is difficult to go contrary to the national grain and the system of cultural values by arguing for toleration. In response, one may say that if one is to work for socialism as an ideal which must overturn deep national habits, why not at the same time work for tolerance as a moral principle?

A familiar Marxist objection to tolerance is that like all moral principles it is part of the superstructure of a society, a reflection of the underlying forces and relations of production, and hence especially related to the level of development of liberal bourgeois societies. I think it a great mistake and a disservice to argue that *all* moral principles are simply reflective of the mode of production, or class-related, or even expendable in the revolutionary struggle. There are, in my judgment, common humanistic principles that transcend their social origins, or at least ought to be treated as having important functions irrespective of the social structure. Toleration is one such principle. It must not be considered in purely formal terms, however, for there are societies that preach it but do not practice it. If tolerance is to be effective, centralized economic or political control of the media of communication must be minimized. In capitalist societies every effort by economic interests to control or monopolize the media must be opposed and *de facto* monopolies must be broken into smaller units. In socialist societies the ministries of information and education should be independent of political and ideological control, and the right of opposition to official policies in the mass media and elsewhere should be legally recognized. A community should not be restricted to one point of view, whether it be that of a dominant economic class, political party, or bureaucratic group; otherwise to claim that toleration of various points of view exists is to mouth nonsense. Last and most important, reprisals—whether by economic sanctions, political intimidation, imprisonment, or worse—should not be exercised against those who express heretical concepts or nonconformist moral values. Where fear is present, criticism gives way to fawning and objective evaluation to cant.

Despite these ideas, there are doubtless some who remain unconvinced, who believe that patent falsehood (such as black magic or astrology) should not be permitted, or that wicked beliefs (in genocide or racism, for example) should not be condoned. Must we not respond that, considering the long-range good of society, the dangers of intolerance are far greater than the open expression of divergent beliefs which may be openly combated? It is better to suffer expressions of falsehood and evil than to attempt to stamp them out; the cure is worse than the disease. I reiterate that this does not mean we should approve of every value or belief; nor that we should suspend criticism. We should battle ideas rather than suppress them. The societies in which the principle of tolerance functions truly will rely upon argument and persuasion rather than upon force as the chief method of social change. It will be based upon appreciation of the individual's uniqueness and dignity, and his value as a member of society. There are other important social values—of community and shared experience—that we need to enunciate. Does our adherence to the principles of libertarianism and tolerance mean that we condone any style of life? Do we, for example, consider pornography, prostitution, homosexuality, or heroin addiction to be good, worthwhile, or beyond criticism? Should we say that if we reject a supernatural basis of life, then all things are permissible and anything goes? Or, as the cynic remarks, "Why not?" My response is that a post-theist or post-puritan humanism does not consider either sexuality or pleasure bad. Indeed, each may be a positive good. Thus pornography is not evil, to be blotted out at all costs; nor is prostitution or homosexuality: *"chacun à son gout."*

Many well-meaning libertarians who have waged campaigns against censorship in the arts are nevertheless appalled by pornographic excesses in "hard-core" movies and magazines that cater primarily to prurient interests. Those who would legalize prostitution are astonished by its increase, and those who believe that the rights of homosexuals should be defended against arbitrary punishment are astounded by the boldness of liberationists who proclaim defiantly that "Gay is good."

I point out again that a distinction should be made between the permissive and tolerant but civilized society. The principle of toleration does not mean that we should approve of all the vagaries of enjoyment, or that we should not seriously criticize excessive fixation on certain pleasures. Many people fear that impressionable young people especially will become licentious and debauched. In defending a libertarian attitude toward social policy, the attempt should also be made to emphasize maturity and responsibility, and the feeling that people ought to develop all their capacities. Thus, toleration imposes a heavy obligation on those responsible for the educational processes of society to stress new dimensions of growth rather than over-emphasizing sex, drugs, or pornography. It is of the greatest importance to encourage healthy and developed personalities in the young.

To say that the state should not harass homosexuals, prostitutes, deviants, or heretics is not to say that it should encourage their activities. I urge moral restraint by the state in matters of private taste and choice, but not moral neutrality in all issues. The state has an important role in human affairs, and even if it should "wither away," other institutions would have the responsibility of fulfilling its functions.

VII / The Principle of Equality

Respect for liberty is a basic principle of humanistic ethics; yet the relationship it bears to the principle of equality and to the demands of the common good is paradoxical. The paradox is that liberty does not exist fully for everyone unless some measure of equality exists as a precondition of its realization; yet excessive stress on efforts to achieve equality often curtails liberty. The good society is one which is able to fuse liberty with equality in some harmonious relationship.

Historically the principle of equality has been defended as the basis of the democratic society, an ideal worthy of our maximum effort. The principle today has renewed power and appeal, with the demand for black power, the cry of the poor and the dispossessed, the determination that women be liberated. Unfortunately, not all those who espouse equality are clear as to what it entails or what is its range of application. It has often been misinterpreted, misapplied, and distorted by passionate devotees. Let us try to clarify it.

EQUALITY AS A DESCRIPTIVE CLAIM

First, equality has been interpreted as making a descriptive claim that all men *are* born equal, and second, as expressing the normative ideal that they *ought* to be treated equally. These claims, though they are often entangled, are separate and distinct. The descriptive claim is factual, to be determined by psychology and biology, by scientific evidence. It is often confused with the normative claim that all human beings are equal—they are *human* and as such have equal dignity and value.

Does "dignity" describe a real property? To argue in this way is to read metaphysical entities into nature, for "dignity" does not exist as separate from those who employ it. Human beings have common needs, face similar problems, have common affections and passions. Individual worth ought therefore to be respected and the claim to dignity recognized. To say that human beings have dignity is to demand that they *ought* to be considered as ends in themselves, and that they are entitled to humane treatment—not that they possess some unobservable, inherent properties. Thus, the equalitarian is making a prescriptive recommendation; he is not offering a description.

Nevertheless, there is at least one descriptive claim that many equalitarians have assumed, based on the extreme view that all human beings are born equal in talent and ability, a premise that seems to me to be profoundly mistaken. The principle of equality is primarily ethical, not descriptive. We should not uncritically assume that all humans are equal in their potentialities.

In what sense are human beings equal in intelligence, aesthetic appreciation, technical know-how, agility? The whole of experience seems to point to the opposite. We all recognize the wide variations in people, dull and bright, active and lazy, warm and cold—the differences are extensive. There are, besides, the tragic accidents of birth—the maimed, the handicapped, the retarded—of which Goethe observed that "it is in her abnormalities that nature reveals herself." But, say the equalitarians, the real issue is not whether humans display different traits and characteristics—they grant that experience shows that they do—but whether, given equal social conditions, they would be more nearly equal in attainment. Are they roughly similar in latent abilities and talents? Are disproportionate levels of achievement due to environment or to genetic differences? Advocates of equalitarianism are convinced that all differences are a result of unjust social conditions and that to ameliorate them would be more nearly to equalize the performance of people. There is, of course, much truth to this view. Man's behavior is conditioned and reinforced by his environment; he is a product of the social forces that converge to form his personality. But is it wholly or largely a question of nurture? To what extent do biological determinants and nature intervene?

Talent

In different eras society has applauded or condemned the poet and romantic, the priest and prophet, the doer and maker. Attitudes depend upon historical contexts and value structures. But do all the Promethean qualities of the human animal depend only upon culture, or are there factors that are genetic in origin? Empirical investigations have demonstrated that genes are important in determining an individual's potential. Yet despite objective findings, there are today commitments to environmentalism and equalitarianism, and prejudices against genetic explanations, that are quasi-religious in nature. This disposition is fed by a commendable desire to ameliorate the human condition, and by a passionate belief that even to concede genetic factors might impede our efforts.

There is, however, considerable evidence indicating that genetic factors are as important as social determinants in explaining many characteristics. In the area of intelligence, for example, researchers have attempted to show—against onslaught by environmentalists—that genetic factors appear to exert a predominant role. And, protests to the contrary notwithstanding, a growing body of research strongly indicates the primary biological basis of intellectual ability.

Psychologists and geneticists have sought to measure intelligence by means of I.Q. tests. The intelligence quotient of a person is based on a concept relating performance to age. If a child outperforms his peers, he is said to be bright; if he underperforms, he is probably dull. If his underperformance is very great, he may be said to be retarded. An average performance is 100. Binet and his successors in I.Q. testing research assumed that mental growth is consecutive and cumulative; that a child who has mastered certain items at a given age will probably continue to develop at the same rate, as he matures. At some point during adolescence the individual stops acquiring new intellectual powers. I.Q. tests, if properly framed, are designed to transcend the limits of culture; they are not supposed to reflect rote memory or the product of schooling, but comprehension, mental alertness, speed, the ability to see relations and solve problems.

Does environment or heredity determine how well a person will perform on such tests? The environmentalist believes that the performance is largely based on nurture. He proposes behavioristic techniques in compensatory education to correct deficiencies in background. In particular, he believes it is the first few years of a child's life that are all-important if he is later to master problems of symbolic and cognitive relationships. Hence, according to the environmentalist, it is important to provide an enriched environment early in life and to sustain it by social and educational opportunities. There is much truth to these claims; in many cases the latent abilities of disadvantaged youth and problem children can be brought forth. On the other hand, there is considerable evidence pointing to the presence of innate structures that are based upon the inbreeding of genetic stocks.

One test of the genetic hypothesis is by the comparison of the intellectual ability of identical twins who, equipped with similar genetic endowment, were raised in different families. The evidence strongly suggests that there are only minor differences in how well the twins perform, even though they may have been raised in quite dissimilar social environments.

Arthur R. Jensen, in his controversial articles in the *Harvard Educational Review* and *Behavior Genetics*,[1] surveys four major studies of identical twins who were reared in separate homes. Most of the twins were separated in the first few months of life and almost all for two years; 122 pairs were studied. Being identical twins, they had

[1] See especially, "How Much Can We Boost I.Q. and Scholastic Achievement?" *Harvard Educational Review*, XXXIX (Winter, 1969) pp. 1-123. See also Arthur R. Jensen, *Genetics and Education*, N. Y., Harper and Row, 1972.

identical genetic inheritances, but their environments were widely different. Yet the I.Q.'s of the twins correlated by about 85 per cent, much higher than those of fraternal twins or ordinary brothers and sisters in the same families. Twins raised apart differed on the average approximately 7 points in I.Q. Any two people chosen at random differ about 17 points. This suggests a stronger correlation between I.Q. and kinship than between I.Q. and environment. Conversely, foster children of different backgrounds raised in the same family manifest wide ranges of intellectual ability. Extensive measurements also indicate that the more closely related, genetically, two people are, the greater the correlation between their I.Q.'s. Indeed, Jensen concluded that the genetic or heritability factor is about 80 per cent and that only 20 per cent is left to environmental conditions, including factors such as illness or prenatal care.

All sorts of objections have been raised against I.Q. tests. It is said that all they measure is how well one does on an I.Q. test, or that they express the biases of the tester, or that they reflect white middle-class cultural norms. Moreover, it is said, I.Q. tests measure only some of the abilities involved in the intellectual attainment of a person, and some capacities are left out—such as time perception, color discrimination, memory, accuracy of bodily movements, co-ordination, effort, motivation, and so on. I do not wish to discuss extensively here the merits or demerits of these claims. My point is that there is a large body of *prima facie* evidence that indicates: (a) some human characteristics are inherited, and (b) there is wide diversity in the range of characteristics that appear among individuals.

The lessons of common experience reinforce an awareness of the relationship between blood and what we are. We do not contest the genetic inheritance of physical characteristics, skin, hair, eye color, body structure, and so on. There is extensive evidence of the inheritance of other abilities, such as musical talent. Yet largely because of a new, virtually religious attitude about environmentalism these elementary points need restating. A normative value—that humans ought to be treated equally—has been allowed to prejudice our scientific examination of evidence and our explanatory hypotheses of how and why people function the way they do. In certain contexts we cannot publish contrary views: As anti-Lysenkoism in the Soviet Union suffered at the hands of Marxist ideology, so Jensen, Herrnstein, and others have often had a difficult time in the United States in publishing these views, as has H. J. Eysenck in Great Britain. A well-meaning humanitarianism has been allowed to intimidate free inquiry and to threaten objective discussion of the evidence. One may argue, however, that this so-called humanitarianism is inverted: Unless we know why a child is dull or retarded our approach toward him may be mistaken and our remedial efforts may be in the wrong direction.

I am concerned here less with marshalling all the evidence of the inherited characteristics of man than with its moral implications for the principle of equality. We may safely infer that individuals manifest wide variations in abilities. If this is the case, the moral issue is how they should be treated. Does the principle of equality still prevail? My answer is in the affirmative. But how and in what sense? It is time that we seek to define equality as a normative rule.

EQUALITY AS A NORMATIVE PRINCIPLE

It should be clear from the above that the principle of equality is not a description of what human beings are, except in the most general sense. They are diverse in their talents, interests, needs. Rather, the principle is prescriptive or normative; it says that humans *ought* to be treated in a certain way, that they are entitled to certain minimal rights because of certain basic similarities, without the implication, however, that they are always to be viewed identically or uniformly: It is not egalitarian. It does not mean that the goods of society ought to be equally divided. Humans are not simply duplicates of each other, nor can they be equalized as if they were, for that would mean the rule of mediocrity in society and the consequent destruction of qualitative excellence. Hence, the principle of equality as a normative ideal must allow for the differential treatment of human beings; if it doesn't it will debase and destroy individual personality.

What, then, does or should equality mean? First, that legal and social rules ought to be applied *impartially*. This involves a doctrine of fairness. All humans are to be treated alike before the law. They are entitled to due process and just application of the law. We should not make invidious distinctions or exceptions based upon privilege, power, wealth, origin, or birth. Each person is to count as one, equal in value, dignity, and worth. Each life is as precious as any other. No distinctions of quality or of value in humans should be allowed as a basis of discrimination. But equality means more. We have certain rights with respect to society and our fellow man; we expect equal treatment from the state and its rules, and equal consideration in their application. Unearned privilege should not prejudice an individual's rights. The needs, values, interests, foibles and idiosyncracies of each person ought to be tolerated, appreciated, respected. More crucially, the principle of equality demands (a) the liberation of the individual from restrictive and debilitating laws and social practices, freedom to do what he wants; and (b) that the state or society provide those minimal conditions that are necessary for individuals to fulfill whatever needs, interests, and potentialities they have.

The principle here is *equal opportunity,* a chance to prove ourselves, to demonstrate our mettle, to work for the goods and the rewards of society on equal terms. It does not imply that all men should have the right to share in all things in the same way; only that the rules of the game be fairly applied and that there be no obstacles in the way of individual achievement. What the principle insists upon negatively is the right to mobility—in the social system, in occupation, and in improving the circumstances of life. It means that no member of any group—racial, ethnic, sexual, etc.—should be discriminated against on that basis, whether for a job, admittance to a university, or acceptance in a neighborhood.

The state or society must provide minimum aid to those who cannot provide for themselves. The moral imperative is that the basic needs of human beings be assured satisfaction by the state. Where a society has sufficient resources, no individual should be allowed to starve, to suffer illness or disease for want of proper medical care, or be disadvantaged in obtaining an education. Equality, welfare, and justice go hand in hand, conjoining freedom from hunger with adequate medical care, old-age assistance, educational and cultural opportunity, protection and security against danger. I am not arguing that society ought routinely to satisfy basic needs. It is far better for each to provide for himself, and that all contribute their share of effort, both for their own and for the common good. Only where people are rendered unable to do so by the complex nature of economic or social conditions do they have a moral claim on society not to let them starve or perish. What constitutes basic needs and a minimum standard of living is of course relative; levels of aspiration are always rising. The principle of equality says only that the fundamental needs of an individual are those required for his health and development and should be made available. Equality should be regarded as comparative and proportional, not egalitarian and uniform; it should recognize the unequal nature of the needs and interests of us all and hence of our satisfactions. It is therefore imperative that the principle of liberty not be impaired in the application of equality. It should be obvious that the demand for equality must not entail undue expropriation, exploitation, or restriction of individual freedom in the name of the common good; nor must it affect incentive or the exercise of creative imagination and invention, all the elements necessary if society is to thrive and individuals are to realize the fullness of being. Many people, the young in particular, properly sense the false opposition and rivalry in a competitive system and are sensitive to the need for developing the virtues of cooperation rather than competition, a sense of community rather than of rivalry. But, in opposing excessive competition, we must not diminish the possibility of leadership based upon achievement and excellence. A good life for mankind may be made possible only by recognizing and encouraging talent.

But if a division of labor and the existence of elites cannot be entirely eliminated, they should be shaped by the vision of an open society, in which there is opportunity for all to contribute and to excel each in his own way. Status and occupation should not be based upon power or prejudice, but upon proven merit. Thus, most thriving societies recognize and applaud achievement—the strong or dominant person, the gifted genius, the exceptional talent; they should continue to do so in the future. Otherwise, talent would languish and society lose the benefit of its contribution.

It may be that the true class society, as Plato thought, should be based on talent and achievement alone; but there should not be wide disparities in wealth; none should enjoy luxuries while others do without necessities. All minimal needs should be satisfied where society has attained a high enough standard of living. It may be true, as some say, that poverty and social class are due in part to under-achievement and a lack of talent. This of course runs counter to liberal doctrine which maintains that poverty has social causes and social cures. Yet some people are unable, for a variety of reasons—illness, under-education, enforced apathy—to achieve a decent standard of living or self-confidence. If talent and an elite are at the one end of the scale, failure of the poor may be at the other.

Selection by merit is often criticized. Universities that apply high standards of admission and graduation are condemned as undemocratic bastions of privilege. Professors who require certification are sometimes accused of being part of oligarchical centers of power. Is the existence of an elite based upon talent and achievement undemocratic, contrary to the will of the majority? In any democratic society can "all of the people all of the time" control all of the decisions? To argue for this is a crude distortion of the democratic ethic. Democracy embraces both freedom and equality, but unless it makes room for proven merit it is bound to fail and to be replaced by more efficient totalitarian controls.

GROUP EQUALITY

These problems become even more complex when they are moved from considerations of the rights of individuals to those of societal groups, and the distinctions made are on the basis of race, ethnicity, or sex. If there is a wide variation in talent among individuals, are there also variations among racial and ethnic groups? And if so, what does this portend for the principle of equality? Many dedicated environmentalists are convinced, for example, that if blacks achieve at a reduced level of performance, it is due to the deprivation caused by a history of white racism. Hence equality is appealed to as the means by which to redress injustice. What light can be thrown on the question whether the underperformance of blacks or other minority groups is due primarily to social causes? Are strong genetic components also present, as Jensen, Herrnstein, and Eysenck argue in regard to Negro intelligence? How will these considerations affect the principle of equality?

To this writer, the environment/heredity controversy as it applies to racial and ethnic groups is still an open question. Many democrats hope that the genetic explanation for racial differences will be proved wrong and that an environmental account will prevail. But what if those who maintain that there are genetic differences between racial and ethnic groups prove to be right? How will this affect our desire to build a just and humane society?

My response is that whatever the outcome of this inquiry, *it should not invalidate the principle of equality*. For although racial and ethnic stocks may differ on achievement and I.Q. tests, for example, there is still wide variance *among individuals* within each group. One cannot argue from a class to each of its members without committing the logical fallacy of distribution. It is obvious that Swedes, for example, as a group tend to be blond, but this does not mean that every Swede will be blond. Therefore, because a racial group happens on the whole to do less well on I.Q. tests than other racial groups, it surely does not follow that every member of that group will underperform members of other groups, or vice versa. Matters are even more complicated: we know that there is no such thing as a pure racial or ethnic stock, especially with the widespread historical fact of intermarriage. But it is the individual that counts, not the group, and all individuals are entitled to equality of opportunity in expressing their talents.

The moral argument for equality of consideration is strong. Parents in a family of several children naturally recognize enormous differences among them in character, ability, aspiration, interest, and intelligence. Yet no one would deny that parents should love each or their children no matter what their individual differences and demonstrate equal concern for them. Similarly, in the family of mankind, any racial or ethnic discrimination is unjustified.

Traditionally it is the racist who does not consider individuals as individuals but labels them in terms of group classification. Unfortunately, many egalitarians today also engage in group thinking. In an effort to ameliorate the conditions of certain disadvantaged groups egalitarians have recently come up with an "affirmative action" program, which establishes quotas. And certain agencies of government —notably the Department of Health, Education and Welfare and the Department of Labor—have systematically attempted to apply this policy. This group theory of equality maintains that each group in society should be represented in each profession and activity in proportion to its percentage of the general population. If a group is underrepresented in an area the conclusion is that this must be due to discrimination, since it is assumed that all groups are equal in ability and talent. The underlying principle here is proportional representation.

Is it just to afford special compensation to certain groups because they have suffered discrimination? Yes, say liberal environmentalists, in order to redress injustice we should try to achieve balance. If any groups are genetically handicapped, should they have special treatment? We give aid to those with diseases which require extensive medical treatment; why should not large sums be expended in schooling minorities so that they may utilize their potentialities? We know that bright persons who underachieve can be overtaken by average ones who are motivated and work hard. Many say that the very arguments being used now against blacks and other minorities were once used against Jews, Italians, and Irish Catholics, and were proved wrong. Should not the same considerations be applied to blacks? Won't they overcome their present situation and excel in the future.

But not every case of underrepresentation is attributable to prejudice; there may be a variety of reasons, cultural and genetic, why certain groups tend to predominate in some professions. Insistence upon proportional representation can have dangerous consequences, for if some groups are underrepresented in certain areas, others may be overrepresented. One imagines zealots demanding that those groups which exceed percentage norms in the professions or in the universities be proportionately reduced. If Jews, for instance, make up only three per cent of the population and are highly visible in the professions, or Episcopalians and Presbyterians occupy key positions in society beyond their population ratios, should their roles be reduced?

A quota system in such matters is discrimination in reverse. Its fallacy is that it does not consider individual merit, but awards preferential treatment to groups of people based upon accidents of birth. If the principle of equality were to prevail, individuals would not need preference as a way of righting the errors of the past. Perhaps the quota system was necessary as a temporary phase of the struggle for equal rights. But if it were to become permanent the consequences might be disastrous, not only in undermining standards of competence, but in its effect upon those for whom exceptions are made. Should any of those who were part of a quota drop out in disappointment or inadequacy, the inevitable bitterness would be explosive. And any groups bypassed for preferential treatment would doubtless explode in resentment. Social harmony could not long survive on such a basis.

If the geneticists who believe that heredity outweighs environment as the chief factor in behavior prove to be right, however, our social policies would naturally have to be altered. We should continue to do all we can to improve performance, not simply by modifying the environment, but also by genetic means: for instance, by encouraging people in the professions to have more children and those with lower I.Q.'s to have fewer, by a policy of intermarriage and miscegenation that encourages the mingling of racial and ethnic groups, and by bio-genetic counselling. Such approaches must be considered since there may indeed be some degree of dysgenics now occurring. Perhaps we also need to exert effort in research to develop chemical substances and drugs that will improve memory, and the analytical and conceptual functions of the mind.

We must insist that the categories of "inferior" and "superior" not be applied either to individuals or groups. All humans have equal dignity and worth. Society may prize certain contributions to the common good as "better" than others, but this should never imply that others are "inferior." The lesson that must be emphasized above all is that no matter what their backgrounds, all human beings should be given equal opportunity as individuals to achieve whatever they are capable of. Any policy of discrimination or preference based upon race or other irrelevant considerations is unjustified.

EQUAL RIGHTS FOR WOMEN

Equal rights have also been justifiably advocated for women. The explanation for several inequalities offered by environmentalists here, too, is at least open to question. Although there are many distinguished women, there are many fields of endeavor in which on the whole women have not attained distinction. They are insufficiently represented in law, medicine, government, business, the arts and sciences; indeed, they have been virtually excluded from most of the positions of power in society. Why? Certainly, in most societies, girls from the very earliest age are taught to be passive, to stay at home, while boys are encouraged to seek a profession, to be aggressive, to achieve in the world. Many assume male supremacy, like white supremacy, to be unquestionable. The whole structure of social expectation subtly undermines a woman's desire to do something with her life, and tends to turn her into an object for the male, whose chief good is as a sex object, wife or mother. Are women equal to men in all forms of talent, the problem being only that they are denied equal opportunity?

The paradoxical condition of modern women, particularly in America and other Western countries, is that while they are restricted to certain functions in society, they enjoy privileges not shared by the male. Women are often condemned either to labor in the home, from morning until night, or to live in idle boredom. This is especially true of the wives of the bourgeois and upper middle classes. While the men work from morning till night, day in and day out, the women often have nothing to do, particularly after the children have grown up, except care for themselves or minister to their man's wants. They have been given a life of luxury and idleness and have become members of a new leisure class. With new labor-saving devices, many are freed from housework but, though they have much free time, they find little to do with it. Life is often humdrum. They become mere symbols of conspicuous consumption.

Many men, moreover, do not want their wives to have a life-work, and will permit them to work only occasionally for special purposes, part time or for a limited period; they prefer to keep their wives in a state of dependence, as symbols of their influence and prestige. Such women often lose a sense of worth and responsibility. They live off their husbands (or ex-husbands), who usually die younger and often leave them substantial means. The women's liberation movement has properly unmasked the demeaning of bourgeois women as baubles and appendages to male pride.

Many men and women have thus worked out a bad bargain. Men are increasingly faced with wives unsatisfied and demanding, always tired, yet full of recrimination and resentment for empty lives. And men are the cause for the despair of such women. Women desire equal dignity and value in their own right, not as mere wards of the males who keep them, and, while more and more women work in contemporary society, they are not afforded the same opportunities and advantages as men. The raising of children can be a full-time business, of significance to the social good, but there are still millions of childless couples and women whose children have grown up, women who should have outlets for the expression of their being.

The movement for women's liberation has highlighted a whole range of injustices that frustrate and undermine a woman's initiative and her desire to be someone besides a mother or wife. The principle of equality prescribes that all discriminatory bars against women be lifted and that new roles be opened up. Women should have the right to marry and divorce as they see fit, to have an abortion or an affair, to have or not to have children, to acquire higher education, to choose a profession or career, to share both in the powers and responsibilities of social life. A free and open society should not only make no distinction on the basis of race or ethnic origins, but also none on the basis of sex.

Moreover, women should use their political and economic power to ensure their emancipation; they should invoke moral persuasion as well as legislative and judicial reform to achieve their liberation. The agenda for equal rights is long overdue. There is no reason, for instance, why women should make up only two per cent of the dentists in the United States, whereas they are seventy per cent in Denmark, or only seven per cent of the physicians, when they comprise twenty per cent in Germany. Since women now comprise more than one-third of the labor force in America, many occupations and careers hitherto closed to them should be opened up; and obviously they should receive equal pay for equal work.

The first humanist principle—that we seek the fullness of life—applies to every person. Accordingly, women are entitled to realize creative satisfaction and well-being, as free and independent personalities, entitled as well to equality of consideration and opportunity.

Once again, however, we should not confuse a normative policy with a descriptive account. The normative principle of equality does not now fully operate. It should. But even if it did, women would not necessarily achieve, compete, or contribute to society in exactly the same way as men; there are still differences between the sexes.

Women's liberationists in their effort to proclaim equality and insist upon equal treatment have not made a clear case in explaining all the differences in male-female roles. To reiterate an old question, why have there been no women in music comparable to Beethoven, in science comparable to Einstein or Newton, to Aristotle or Kant in philosophy, to Leonardo or Picasso in painting, to Michelangelo in sculpture, to Edison in invention, or Frank Lloyd Wright in architecture? Is culture the sole cause? Is it due to the obstacles to equal access? Are there biological causes as well?

Let us first state the case for environmentalism. Historically, there has been a massive effort to condition women to accept a passive role in society, in relation to men. This inferior status has deep roots within our cultural heritage; it permeates all our institutions, our religious, moral and legal traditions, and our family structures. Women have not been considered equal to men and in the final analysis have been expected to do their bidding. They have been regarded as sexual objects, instruments for male pleasure; and in their primary role within the family, as breeders and bearers of children; as wards of men.

Economic and political institutions in society are generally the exclusive province of males. Where women are admitted to the centers of decision-making, they are invariably in a subordinate role; they receive less income, even for the same work; rarely do they wield great power. There is a basic male prejudice against sharing their roles with women, deeply ingrained in typical male behavior.

What is more damaging is that women, taught to accept inferior status and dependency, in the process often turn against themselves. Because a girl is encouraged to get married, a boy to seek a career, a woman who is more intelligent or creative than her mate may often decide to suppress her talents rather than offend his sensibilities, often out of fear that she will not hold on to him. Granted that women do achieve eminence and distinction in some fields; for most, the world is a man's preserve, where the few women who are admitted to the councils of power are tokens.

For the environmentalist, the cause of woman's demeaning position and lack of advancement is male chauvinism, ingrained in institutional patterns and scarring the female by imposing psychological acquiescence. But, we are told, this need not be the case. Female subservience is not a product of nature, but of nurture. And only when the archaic, restrictive conventions are finally destroyed can women truly fulfill their individual natures.

Is this environmentalist diagnosis of women's role in society accurate? Are there important biological factors that have been overlooked? Why have women been in positions of subservience throughout the history of mankind? Why have there been few instances of females genuinely dominating society? Why should male dominance be virtually universal, preventing women who are otherwise competent from rising to the top? Why do women not play a more decisive role in such a highly mobile society as the United States? Why do they not have a greater role in France, a society that has often overthrown social fashions and sexual taboos? Why not in the Soviet Union, Cuba, China, all countries of revolutionary ferment? Why did women not have a higher position in Athens where the ideal of women's freedom was known and discussed? Plato defended sexual equality in *The Republic,* as did Aristophanes in *Lysistrata.* Mill devastatingly attacked the subjugation of women; why was freedom for women not achieved in Mill's libertarian England?

Women are at least equal to and perhaps more intelligent than men. Obviously men and women in the long evolutionary history of the species were not selectively bred in the same way and so they are perhaps not equal in talent, ability, interest, needs. The problem lies partly in biology. The basic differences between the sexes, rooted in deepest somatic structures, are displayed in various ways. In the act of sexual intercourse when the penis penetrates the vagina one body physically dominates the other. To begin with it involves inflicting pain as the penis rams into the woman's body, as well as pleasurable excitation. In some species the male rapes the female; he forces his attention on her, claws or bites her neck until she submits. In human culture the sexual act is, of course, ramified, with diverse positions and nuances. Although masculine sexuality suggests the active role of penetration and thrust, and the female of passive reception, there is wide variation in sexual behavior—some males are passive, some females active. The many other forms of sexuality, from masturbation to anal and oral stimulation, suggest that rigid sexual norms are difficult to define. The complementary roles of male and female, especially in sexuality related to reproduction, have a significant relation to the physical structures and psychology of the sexes. While that limited part of the male body in which the penis and testicles are concentrated is given to sex, the female's pelvic and hip area is all focused on reproduction and child-bearing, and the menstrual cycle and hormonal level also channel the woman's energies and capacities. During the menstrual flow for example, women tend to be excitable, irritable, high-strung.

Lionel Tiger and Robin Fox in *The Imperial Animal*[5] offer a provocative explanation of the differences between the sexes and their roles in society: In the process of evolution, men became hunters and predators, gathering in packs with other males, searching for prey, stalking and killing, and bringing food back to the cave where the women remained, prepared the food and cared for the children. Not only were men hunters, they were also warriors who protected the family unit or tribe from attack by wild animals or other humans. It was their structure and strength that qualified men for this role. Of 193 living species of apes, monkeys, and man, only the spider monkey has a female sometimes bigger than the male. (A notable exception to male specialization in hunting is to be found in lions.) The rudimentary social organization of the family tribe thus seems to be basically biological, not economic or sociological in origin.

Human males apparently still remain "upper Paleolithic hunters designed for pursuit of game." Indeed almost all of human history has been concerned with hunting, and out of this developed the tendency for males to be capable of violence, aggression, killing, war. Out of this developed also the need for men to work together in hunting parties, and a new kind of comradeship in arms. The tendency to violence and the hunt was intensified by the evolutionary process; for generally it was the dominant, more cunning males who bred. Weaker males were either expelled from the group or killed off, at best remaining subservient until they could compete with the dominant males for hegemony; females usually stayed on the sidelines.

Similar tendencies have been observed in other primates whose social structures correlate with those of human society. Observations of baboons show the existence of a hierarchical class system, with a ranking order and internal discipline, in which the stronger males dominate. In the evolutionary struggle, females had their special role

[5] N. Y., Holt, Rinehart and Winston, 1971.

in the social system. They cared for the young, whom they breast fed and protected from danger. Out of this there developed the mother-child bond that is now essential to normal growth and health. If the infant or child is deprived of a mother's, or surrogate mother's, care, it will not grow normally. This basic biological and psychological condition of health is deeply rooted in the past of the species.

Agriculture and industry, in contrast, are only relatively recent phenomena. The discovery that the tribe did not have to roam to seek food, but could remain in one place, till the soil, gather fruits and vegetables from the harvest, and bake bread, marked a turning point in the emergence of human civilization. With it, the roles of the sexes were drastically altered. The male was no longer the wandering hunter; both males and females were needed to work the land; men tilled the fields; women supplied large families of sons to assist. The comparatively recent development of industrial society uprooted man from his rural existence and created new roles for the wives of an industrial proletariat, the businessman, the executive. Yet though males have long since transcended their existence as hunters, and females their roles as fire-tenders, humans are still endowed with the attributes and characteristics of their hunting lineage. The male is still an efficient biped, with an enlarged cerebral cortex, able to seek out and devour prey in order to survive. The new and dazzling development of an advanced language and culture must be superimposed upon the biological equipment of the predator.

Can humans overcome the limitations of their somatic structures? Should they? Will males forever dominate females as they have since the beginning of the species? Will the male now change because his inherited tools and capacities for hunting are no longer required, because they are residual in modern society? Can sexual roles even be reversed? Should men nurture children, and women become active in the "man's world"?

These difficult questions concern the kind of human beings that we want to create. In speculating about our future, we can imagine bold utopias, but our biological nature is still relatively fixed; we are constrained and limited by it; our potentialities are still rooted in our nature. Our vision of what we want to be may conflict with what we are. Though men and women no longer need to eke out their lives in a hunting economy, they still possess talents related to the earlier mode of existence. They have been selected for it by adaptation, mutation, evolution; they are constrained by species, biology, and history. Egalitarians insist that discernible male-female differences in biological and social functions can be overcome. But to gloss over the intrinsic biological contrasts is foolish.

As already stated, women are at least equal, perhaps even superior, to men in intellectual capacity. (There do seem to be fewer females of subnormal intelligence, while males have seemed to outnumber women in super-intelligence and genius.) The female is able to pick up and learn at an early age, to assimilate verbal skills, to surpass men in I.Q. tests and school work, but though females develop linguistic and cognitive skills early in life, after puberty males seem to surpass them. Men tend to want to intervene in nature and manipulate it for their own use. It is the male who is predominately the tool maker and user. While females create primarily by giving form to life within the womb, men create in the external world. Man ejaculates; woman absorbs and conserves what man gives. The Prometheus model in the last analysis is a heroic male figure, able to use intelligence and reason to reorder his universe so that it fits his needs and interests. The male has the courage to master something when others say it cannot be done. The masculine nature is less likely to take "No" for an answer. It is the male who is the inventor and discoverer, the explorer and investigator, the doer and maker in the world.

The form that the active male principle takes is of course dependent upon social conditions and values. There are males who retreat from demands made upon them, and females who fill the man's role. Audacity is surely not an exclusive male province; it is at the very center of the human drama, of happiness and achievement. It defines the species, and is only magnified in the male. In the many ramifications of sexual differences—in function, behavior, biology, and psychology—male and female cooperate with and complement each other. The world man builds is not for himself alone, but for his loved ones, his wife and his children; and woman shares in building the structure of family, helping to maintain her offspring and her mate. While male and female are both capable of creativity, the major difference in the expression of it seems to lie in the male's ability to conceptualize, the female's ability to intuit. In the fields that call upon abstract conceptualization and formal reasoning, the male generally has been the conceiver of the future. In the female, emotional responsiveness, immediacy, warmth, patience, compassion, intuitive insight have been the dominant gifts. The defender of tranquility and peace, she provides the bond of cooperative society, and of course holds the family together.

It is not entirely the case that the male dominates the female physically; the female cooperates by yielding herself. The division of labor in their lives together is rooted in sexuality.

Many of those allied with women's liberation have stressed the tendency of males to be warlike and aggressive, maintaining that if roles were switched and women acquired political and economic power, there would be a better chance for the virtues of pacifism to emerge. In this they apparently concede a basic difference between the sexes. Men tend to go to war or, as William James observed, to participate in certain moral equivalents of war—competition, in business, politics, and sports. Are utopians correct when they claim that women would be a moderating influence in power? Since man, the predator, has made a mess of the contemporary world, perhaps we ought indeed to give woman a chance. Some women have, of course, held political power, in most cases inherited by queens and empresses, and in some cases earned, by such leaders as Golda Meir and Indira Gandhi. More often than not, however, when women command vast power they seem to behave in ways similar to those of men, often of necessity aggressively. Perhaps the world of men constrains their feminine qualities; perhaps even hormonal fluids are affected; perhaps it is out of a need to prove themselves that they act aggressively.

When in the past, the farmer replaced the hunter, a new system of values emerged. The Christian ethic appeared when there was a great need to tame the predator. It stresses passivity and acquiescence; Jesus enunciated a message of love and forgiveness to replace violence and aggression. When mankind needed in its history to be domesticated, to return to some form of pastoral tranquility, Christianity both reflected and encouraged this need. But that ethic, designed for a comparatively simple life, was not adaptable to modern society, and the Protestant ethic which encouraged action, competition, fortitude was much more compatible with the new conditions.

We are now at another turning point; we need to transcend our past—not the rural period, but our recent industrial mode. A theistic morality is irrelevant in the present context; the sociological and ethical structures of rural life and industrial civilization are breaking down. As we enter a new epoch of post-industrial technology, scientific imagination promises us a new world of unparalleled power and possibility, yet our primeval roots still constrain what we can do. For women, hunting, rural and industrial society provided a station, duties, labor. Today, women are increasingly finding themselves without significant roles, particularly in childless homes or homes where the children have grown up and left. We must transform our society so that women may again discover significant and enriching ends by which they may be fulfilled, not alienated. Women can no longer exist only to satisfy men's needs or to raise families; they must develop their own modes of being. Since we no longer live in a hunting society, where the division of labor was fixed, or in a rural society where big households and family chores took all of a woman's time, and since we are moving out of an industrial society, where women have begun to lose their traditional roles, they must be able to transcend the limitations of their past. Is the solution to the problem of male/female roles that human beings must overcome what they have been? Although our nature is not fixed, can we go contrary to those needs that have been present since the origin of our species, and still be happy? Should the fact that men were hunters and women tended the hearth in the past determine how humans behave in the future?

What is at issue here is the transformation of sexuality itself. If the human species is able to overcome sexual distinctions by means of biological and genetic manipulation, should it do so? Can the male/female problem be resolved, for example, by developing a unisexual or gender-neuter human being? Would this not be the end of the mystery and joy of sexual experience? And is not sexuality essential to our being human?

At present we need to restrict population. Not all women should breed. Those who do, moreover, will soon be able to "bear" their babies *in vitro,* in test tubes or the wombs of other animals, without the need for implantation in their own bodies. Given this development, a chief role of women will be bypassed. Will women still be necessary as mothers to nourish and raise their young after they are born, or will other social forms take over that historic role as well? Will society, for example, entirely replace the family unit (as in *Walden Two*) by trained professional educators who are specialists in bringing up children? If this should happen, what will the role of women be? Will they be dependent upon men and continue to share a life-work with them? Or will they find new occupations and careers, appropriate to their own personalities? Will new relationships between the sexes and new forms of marriage and cohabitation prevail?

Perhaps the recent interest in deviant sexuality, such as lesbianism, is a reflection not simply of individuals but of a tendency in the species. Perhaps bisexuality expresses a new stage of social and biological evolution in which masculine/feminine differences are being blurred. Even now, it is often difficult to discern sexual differences in hair style, dress, and manners. Undoubtedly there are cultural and psycho-biological causes of bisexuality such as social abnormalities and hormonal deficiencies, but the bisexual form may be symptomatic of our future. It is increasingly possible for the human species to control the direction of its evolution, to determine sexual and other characteristics of its offspring, to decide whether the chromosomes will be female (xx) or male (xy), what the color of the hair or eyes will be, whether masculine or feminine traits will dominate, and so on.

Given these possibilities, it is essential that we determine where we are going. Shulamith Firestone, in her book *The Dialectics of Sex*[6], recognizes that there are biological, not simply sociological, differences between the sexes, and she advocates biological transformation to make sexual equality a reality. Perhaps this is mere science fiction gone wild. But we must ask the moral question: should we, even if we could, change sexuality, the source of so much human pleasure and satisfaction? Should we do it simply to make sexual equality possible? Would this not be too heavy a price to pay?

We return to our original consideration. If men have overachieved in some fields and women underachieved in some, the reasons are partially attributable to social and cultural discrimination, and there are genetic and other biological causes as well. A doctrine of equality commits the descriptivist fallacy when it fails to allow

6 N. Y., William Morrow, 1970.

for biological differences and tries to force a quota system upon society to compensate for developments that may result from them. In committing this fallacy, many advocates of women's liberation are expressing an anti-woman bias. Do they really envy penises? Do they not demean the qualities of femininity by seeking to emulate the characteristics of the masculine form? Should they not appreciate and cherish feminine qualities for their own sake without seeking to transform or deny them?

The principle of equality is fundamentally normative; it should not be taken for an oversimplified descriptive theory. It recommends that we treat individuals as *individuals,* that all false barriers based upon sexist or racist discrimination be lifted. Women who wish to enter the professions, to have careers, to develop the arts of leisure, or to raise families should have the right to do so; and in the world of commerce they should be rewarded according to their merits, without bias. Increasingly, women enter professions heretofore closed to them. Fair treatment, equality of consideration and opportunity, must be basic in a democratic society. Where there are differences, given our biological limits, we ought not to compel men or women to deny the differences or accept uniformity. We ought rather to respect the virtues of femininity and masculinity and all the varieties and nuances of individuality.

Those who are committed to the principles of equality and liberty should have no illusions about what they mean or how they will work out. Though they are designed to make possible a more creative life for individuals, they will not bring utopia. And when cries for liberty and equality are disguised precepts of religious dogma, they assume nonsensical forms. Though we may be committed to the realization of freedom and equality as part of the democratic ethic, we must be skeptical of their uncritical applications or of claims that they will lead to salvation.

VIII / The Democratic Ethic

THE MEANING OF DEMOCRACY

Democracy is still the most radical social philosophy in the world today—radical because there are so many opposed to it and so few who genuinely understand or believe in it, and because, if adopted, it would mean a fundamental change in human institutions. Nevertheless it is espoused by people on all sides of the political spectrum. Liberals praise democracy; so do conservatives and reactionaries; even Marxist communists defend what they call "people's democratic republics." Democracy, like other noble ideals, is thought to confer virtue by association. Yet not all those who pay lip service to it are democrats. Democracy has been betrayed by totalitarians and humanitarians of all kinds—by those who believe in government for the people, if not necessarily of or by them—and has been undermined by apostles of the far right and the far left.

One source of this confusion is that many of those who appeal for democracy are uncertain of its nature, or else choose to misapply it.

156

What is "democracy"? How is it to be applied? Are there any limits that a society calling itself democratic should not exceed? What is essential to democracy?

THE ETHICAL DIMENSIONS OF DEMOCRACY

The term "democracy" may be used in different senses. We talk of political, economic, racial, social democracy. The essential factor, in my judgment, is that democracy expresses an ethical dimension: It advocates first and foremost a normative ideal—one that recommends how we shall treat people, and how we should live and work together as individuals in community. Although the democratic ideal has many different interpretations and applications, it cannot be implemented without recognition of its basic moral foundations.

What are the moral principles that it expresses? As we have seen, the democratic philosophy involves at the very least a commitment to the principles of liberty and equality. But as we also have seen, if the principle of liberty is overemphasized, it may lead to an extreme laissez-faire individualism or anarchism that may deny the rights of others; it may ignore the need for equality of treatment; and it may lead to an unjust society in which large sections of the population are disenfranchised socially and economically and excluded from the good things of life. Indeed, the principle of freedom if allowed to reign alone may eventually lead to an exclusive class society in which some individuals or groups would possess power, while large numbers of people are bypassed or excluded from effective involvement. On the other hand, an egalitarian society which is excessively protective of equal rights might so restrict individual freedom that the right of choice and initiative would be thwarted. Societies that emphasize egalitarianism and ignore libertarianism generally tend to become totalitarian, willing to trample on freedoms of thought, action, and dissent.

In its concern for the worth and dignity of the individual democracy recognizes his right to do what he wishes and restricts undue interference in the sphere of individual choice and action. It provides the opportunity and conditions for personal realization and growth.

The democratic ethic recognizes that insofar as we respect an individual's right to personal freedom, we contribute not only to his growth but to our own; insofar as we can appreciate others we can learn to share their stores of experience, wisdom, truth. In being tolerant of diversity, the democratic approach enlarges our horizons for discovery and insight; it permits creative growth in the community, for it eliminates undue limitations on uniqueness. Insofar as I am willing to listen to another, to consider him as a being entitled to equal consideration and fair treatment, I contribute to both my development and his.

The democratic ethic is also based on the idea of freely given consent; its institutions strive as nearly as possible to base their policies on the consent of the greatest number of people. This consent is not mere acquiescence; it must be freely given in active approval of the main directions being taken and confidence in the key officials who are to carry them out.

Consent alone is never enough. We should always seek to enlist real participation in the affairs of the state, the sharing of power and responsibility on all levels. Since each one has an equal stake in society and in life, each should have a commensurate role. The true democrat has some measure of faith in the "ordinary man," in his ingrained wisdom and practical judgment, particularly in that which concerns his self-interest. The democratic ethic denies that any group or class has special knowledge or moral virtue that enables it to judge better what is good for others than they can judge for themselves. No claim to power based upon privilege, wealth, prestige, birth or background entitles any group to exercise rule.

There are, of course, many interpretations of cooperative participation. Some believe that democracy requires consensus, even unanimity. Yet, although in democratic decisions one tries to arouse wide, if possible unanimous, support for a policy or program, it is rarely if ever attained. In small groups where decisions are made face-to-face in daily encounter, it may be possible to reach consensus; the method is persuasion and negotiation. In a large social context, with diversity of opinion, the next best thing is majority rule. Majorities are often lumbering and in error, but they are fairer to a greater number of interests than the minority, even though the minority may be correct.

What is crucial for democracy is the method by which decisions are reached. The most desirable method is that of peaceful deliberation, discussion, persuasion, the widest possible dialogue between opposing conceptions. In recognizing that no individual or group may possess all the truth, democracy leaves open the possibilities for the clash of competing views, and thrives on heresy and nonconformity.

BASIC COMMITMENTS

Of course, democracy can only survive if its citizens abide by certain rules. Provided that you are willing to listen to me or to those who represent me, and possibly be persuaded to change, I will try to convince you, says the democrat, but if I cannot I will go along in general with what the majority wants. What is essential is the willingness to negotiate differences and to reach common ground. If the democratic method of shared decision-making is to be effective, it presupposes that certain concomitant policies and procedures be present. What is of first importance is that there be a common framework of values and ideals; for a democracy to operate there must be some consensual agreement that the ethic of democracy is just and humane. Those who live in the community may dissent from current policies and pursue a plurality of life styles or hold different belief systems; yet they should have some intelligent commitment to the framework, that is, to the method by which social change is made possible, policies are enacted, and leaders are selected. If large sections of the population do not believe in democracy and are willing to abandon it for a more efficient, more orderly, or what seems to promise a more just system, the democratic ethic will break down; and if in an underdeveloped nation, there is no heritage of democratic values, it is hardly likely to accept democracy, which presupposes some allegiance to common values. The serious problem that some Western countries now face is that large sections of the populace, whether of the New Left or Old Right, are no longer really loyal to the moral premises of democracy.

AN OPEN SOCIETY: FREE EDUCATION AND INFORMATION

Public knowledge and access to truth are pre-conditions of a democratic society. If public decisions are to be made wisely, it is important that state secrets be at a minimum and truly concern national security.

Democracy requires some system of universal education. This does not mean that all men are entitled to pursue programs in all fields, or be admitted to all institutions of higher education without qualification; as we have seen, rewards should depend upon merit. What it does mean is that basic opportunities are to be available for all. As John Dewey recommended, an appreciation for democratic values should be developed in the young, the capacity for shared experience and toleration, and most vitally, the cultivation of the arts of intelligence. For only an informed citizenry, capable of distinguishing the true from the false, is the most reliable safeguard for a democracy.

If the citizens are to reach their decisions wisely, moreover, it is also essential that there be free access to *all* sources of inquiry. Thus, freedom of opinion, research, investigation, and publication are essential: The key public value is cooperative inquiry. This is not possible where there is no marketplace in which ideas can be examined. We have seen how in totalitarian societies the ministries of information control the sources of information—radio, TV, cinema, magazines, newspapers, book publishing, education; and so we must fundamentally oppose those societies in which elementary freedoms are denied, and not be misled by those who label as "democratic" the communist societies closed to free inquiry. In capitalist and quasi-democratic societies in the West, on the other hand, it is vital that large commercial interests not be allowed to control the mass media. A genuine threat to freedom of information in the United States has emerged because the control of television is concentrated in only a few national networks and only two or three wire services predominate—an unfortunate narrowing of points of view. The development of large conglomerates in the book, newspaper, and magazine publishing fields must also be viewed with alarm.

The problem of free communication and access to information is of course related to economics. If democracy is to be effective it is necessary that the media be free of undue control by advertising merchants. It is said that the mass media, based upon the profit motive, need to sell their services to advertisers if they are to be supported. But from the standpoint of the public interest, the first duty of the media should be to inform and only secondarily to profit. There can be no quibbling on this point and no compromise. We would surely complain if our public school system were run primarily for profit rather than for service. It is one thing to have the profit motive rule in manufacturing automobiles or selling shoes; it is quite another to allow it to dominate in the sensitive area of ideas, the mainstays of a viable democratic society.

Democracy cannot operate where there is fear or intimidation of opinion, nor where pressures compel people against their better judgment. In dictatorships the threat of imprisonment and torture effectively prevents expression of ideas, but other forms of sanctions operate more subtly in a democracy to undermine an individual's courage—fear of losing security or status, of ecclesiastical pressure threatening excommunication or penance, of social discrimination or racial prejudice.

An increasing peril is the misuse of the mass media. Here too we have seen how dictatorships use them to indoctrinate, to keep people misinformed and docile. The mass media are used in subtle or unscrupulous ways by advertisers, who by conditioning techniques persuade consumers to buy shoddy products. When such techniques are used to sell the presidency or other political offices, the whole fabric of a democratic polity is undermined. I am not objecting to advertising *per se* as the informed description of products and services, nor surely to the use of the mass media by contenders for political office. What I do condemn is the increasingly abusive manipulation of the air waves by political hucksters. The members of modern society are consumers but they are also citizens and the mass media should not be allowed to cater to one role while they neglect the other. I am not arguing for state control of advertisers and the mass media—we have seen how political power can be as offensive as economic power—but for democratic mechanisms of regulation and of support. Consumer unions and groups, for example, should also be allowed to advertise and analyze products sold through the mass media. It is essential that the consumer have some power over what is fed to him and that corporate organizations be democratized and regulated so that the public interest will never be overlooked.

INDIVIDUAL AND MINORITY RIGHTS

If democracy is rule by the people, can the people ever suspend the rights of individuals or of minorities even if they are offensive?

If democracy is rule by the majority, can a majority ever abrogate the rights of those with whom it disagrees? Can it suppress recalcitrant minorities? There is considerable confusion here, even among some of the best-intentioned of democrats: After all, if we agree to abide by the majority decision, how can we intervene when it goes against what we like? Must we not suffer in silence, hoping to persuade the majority to reverse itself?

The majority is not sacred; nor does majority rule remain inviolable under every circumstance. Democracy rests upon still more fundamental principles—liberty, equality, toleration, civil disobedience—which are higher on the scale of values. Majority rule does not have an intrinsic value in itself. It is only a mechanism to ensure conditions of social harmony and peace and is used because it entails fewer risks and dangers to social welfare than other methods of decision-making. Majority rule is justified only because it safeguards individual rights; it must not be used to suppress them; and opposing minorities and individuals have obligations to the majority—not to impose their beliefs by non-democratic means. The protection of minority rights is a pre-condition of any democratic society, in which majorities are free to determine public policy but not to undermine the ethical presuppositions of democracy.

Am I not bringing in a doctrine of natural rights that are prior to political policy? No, I reject any such fiction. Nor do I accept the notion of a social contract. All individual and minority rights are social; they are claims made upon the community, which lay down certain restrictions upon political power. To say that certain liberties and rights should be recognized is to make a normative claim. It is to prescribe or direct future action. How should we regard or treat individuals in society? They are entitled to equal consideration and freedom even if the majority disagrees with them.

How are these principles to be justified? They are not derived from a divine or natural law, nor do they have any special metaphysical status. They are rules offered to govern how we shall behave. They can be justified only by reference to their results. Societies that nourish the rights of individuals and minorities will, in the long run, be happier, more humane, and just. Societies willing to suspend individual rights whenever immediate purposes seem to require it will be liable to disharmony. The respect for those rights is justified because they are more likely to ensure the common good and the conditions whereby individuals may discover the fullness of life.

THE RULE OF LAW

A democratic society is also based upon respect for due process and the rule of law. There are those who indict "legalism" and "parliamentarianism," and who attack the slow-moving character of democratic societies committed to legal processes, in which policies rest upon precedent. There is a temptation for some to prefer rule by fiat in order to get things done rapidly, independently of legal tradition or bureaucratic red tape. Yet if there is one conclusion to be drawn from the history of political and social philosophy, it is the collective wisdom of the law. Plato in *The Republic* wanted philosopher-kings to rule, and to apply their wisdom and knowledge for the social good. Utopianists and totalitarians ever since have decried laws that have stood in their way and have defended "reason" and "revelation." Yet Plato himself recognized in *The Laws* that in the absence of a philosopher-king, laws are the best guarantors of freedom. Alas, such philosopher-kings have not yet been discovered; nor does the easy temptation today to resort to behavioral scientists as our messiahs promise anything better. Laws still seem a more reliable way of running a society. Laws, however, provide us only with general guides for behavior; how they work out depends upon the context. In a just society laws are applied without discrimination. In the absence of law there would be no possibility of security; fear and indecision would be our constant companions. Of course provisions must be allowed for equity in interpreting and adjusting them to new situations. Further, a just society should try to minimize the regulation of our lives, to leave to individual citizens the widest possible latitude; where regulation is necessary, it should be based upon legal development.

A recurrent problem arises when in the name of civil disobedience and equal rights, some partisans flout the law and argue that it is corrupt. They dramatize crime in the ghettoes, minimize its consequences, and explain it by attributing it to unjust conditions. There is of course a good deal of truth to this claim, particularly for disadvantaged minorities who have often been brutalized by excessive police power and denied their rights. We also need to decriminalize much of the law; as the discussion in Chapter VI shows, many so-called criminal offenses ought not to be so considered.

Of course, law does not guarantee freedom. History has taught us how it can be oppressive and arbitrary, especially in fascist or closed societies. The ideal is for laws to come into being and to become modified by the parliamentary process, and to be applied impartially and humanely. If law is essential to a democracy, it is equally essential that it must not become sacrosanct, that it be responsive to the will of the people, and tested by its consequences in action.

THE JUSTIFICATION OF THE DEMOCRATIC IDEAL

The above is a mere outline suggestive of some features of a democratic society. Does such a society exist? Obviously not. Democracy is an ideal and any definition of it must be ideal. Naturally there is a descriptive element in the definition. "Democracy" does not refer to some theoretical entity independent of the real world. Many societies have had democratic features, but none has ever been a pure democracy. Hence the concept is comparative, a standard by which we may criticize, classify, and compare existing states, and a guide and incentive to greater democracy in the future. So the definition of democracy is normative and prescriptive for the development of society, and for the ethical principles by which we may evaluate policies and systems and reform them.

We have recently heard indictments of so-called democratic societies. Young idealists accuse them of being hypocritical and of betraying their ideals in practice—the result of defects in the democratic ideal. It is said that democracy doesn't work; we need something else. But as I have pointed out, no society—not America nor Britain nor the Scandinavian countries nor ancient Athens—has ever fully implemented the democratic ideal. Then how justify continued commitment to democracy? How would we go about proving its efficacy and power?

One should, to begin with, have a mature and realistic attitude about social systems and ideals. Although there has been immense progress in human affairs, only a pure visionary would expect to see all problems solved or utopia achieved. The justification of democracy is always relative, not rooted in metaphysics or science; it cannot have a deductive or necessary proof. The demand for that kind of justification is, like the demand for the justification of life, an expression of religious need. Democracy can only be vindicated practically and empirically. And what of the alternatives—dictatorship, oligarchy, aristocracy? At least democracy has a wider concern for a greater number of people; even the lowliest have a stake in it, and so it has a more extensive appeal. But also, in comparative terms, it provides fewer dangers and fewer negative consequences than other systems. There is always the danger that self-interest may be confused with the common good. Power has corrupted and blinded rulers throughout history to their own imperfections; it is dangerous to entrust power to an individual or group without proper checks and balances. This has been the collective wisdom of human experience. Anti-democratic societies, which award power on the basis of class, wealth, or military force, tend to degenerate into self-interested rule. Since in a democracy those who are responsible can be called to account there is less likelihood of excessive duplicity or cruelty. Of course injustices and mistakes occur in a democracy, but at least where a society is open injustices can be examined by the critical eye of the public.

Consequently, in democratic societies muckraking is an important tradition for exposing graft and corruption, whereas people in totalitarian societies usually live in illusion, far less aware of social problems. It has been said by Marxist critics that America, and other Western democracies, are in decay, whereas the Soviet Union and some Eastern European countries are coalescing and advancing. So it may seem on the surface, but is that not true in part to the fact that the West has some freedom of the press, which tends to dramatize its problems—from alcoholism and crime to political corruption and wiretapping, from poverty to racism, among others? It is universally recognized that totalitarian societies, though they have similar problems, withhold them from public view by controlling the press. We need to be mindful of putting things in perspective. At least, free societies can know about problems which closed societies cannot.

Surely democracy has the potential for the widest realization of happiness for the largest number. It provides the richest soil for both individual development and social cooperation. With a role in society and a stake in the future, man becomes a devoted member of the cause that provides such noble opportunities; his alienation is reduced, his creative commitment and loyalty enhanced. In an age of crisis in religious commitment, democracy is more amenable to meaningful identification with worthwhile goals. It is more likely to be creative and innovative, more receptive to invention and discovery than a closed, hierarchical, or fixed society. Thus, if viewed in terms of desirable consequences, more people will tend to find a more satisfying life on the whole in a democratic system than in a non-democratic one. There are those who have had no experience of freedom, who either go wild when they first taste it or flee in fear and seek to escape it. Democracy presupposes that the experience of freedom in the young will develop an understanding of its responsible application so that it will become ingrained in the mores of the society.

POLITICAL DEMOCRACY

This discussion has been a general one, concerning the ideal normative features of democracy viewed in its ethical and social dimensions. But it is the *way* that these principles work out in practice that is important. Some institutions of a society are democratic, some not. With respect to institutions, most democrats believe that an essential pre-condition for the realization of any genuinely ethical system is political democracy. But many Marxists who claim to be "democratic" deny the importance of this and debunk the definition of liberal political democracy as mere "bourgeois deception."

What is a democratic *political* system? The term "political system" refers primarily to the operations of state and government, the control of decision-making and power. In large nation states, the only feasible method of rule is by means of representation. Although democracy encourages decentralization, enlisting the largest degree of involvement at all levels, some policies cannot be adequately arrived at by a local unit and have to be enunciated for the whole society. The only practical way to implement the democratic philosophy is for the people to delegate power by electing representatives to carry out the main programs. In a large society we cannot elect all the government officials (the United States, for example, has some 12 million government workers), but only key leaders. Nor can the people by means of elections determine all the policies of the state (there are of course many thousands of governmental rules and regulations, many of them highly technical), but only general guidelines. The presumption is that the major policies are fully discussed before they are adopted. Accordingly, the operation of majority rule, though not a "pure" form of democracy, is the most feasible method of expressing the will of the people. Free elections are the necessary ingredient in a democratic polity, local, state, and federal, as well as in the control of political parties.

Concomitant with this is the legal right of the individual not only to disagree but to make known his opposition to leaders and programs. Where there is no right to oppose the government, to submit its policies to critical scrutiny, and to offer alternatives, there is no democracy. One-party states, where leaders are selected by acclamation, where there are no alternative programs available, and no mechanisms for making known the views of those in opposition, are not democratic, even though totalitarians attempt to co-opt the term "democracy."

Democracy allows the representatives of the people the right to exercise some independence and autonomous judgment. But since most citizens do not have the time, energy, or interest to be concerned with every decision, a bureaucracy or elite will often emerge. A democracy therefore functions best when there is some intelligent distrust of leaders—if not of motives, certainly of policies and consequences. Excessive criticism, however, and unwillingness to allow them some latitude in judgment and some authority in acting, will undermine their ability to govern, both on the international and domestic levels. On the other hand, the glorification of leaders is antithetical to a democratic milieu. Many who remain in office for ten or twenty years become removed from the people; unresponsiveness sets in; history has taught us how important it is that leadership be refurbished.

In the last analysis a political democracy can be effective only if its citizens are interested in the affairs of government and participate in it by way of constant discussion, letter writing, free association and publication. In the absence of such interest, democracy will become inoperative; an informed electorate is the best guarantee of its survival.

SOCIAL DEMOCRACY

But to talk about the instrumentalities of *political* democracy would be merely rhetorical, if *social* democracy did not exist along with it. What is social democracy? I wish to focus first on two aspects: (a) the elimination of discrimination, racial, ethnic and sexual; and (b) the destruction of a closed class society.

Democracy requires an *open* society. Political democracy by itself is not a sufficient guarantee that the society will be one. Invidious distinctions drawn between individuals and groups prevent the full realization of the ethics of democracy. The most notorious, as we have seen, are the forms of exclusiveness based upon racial, religious, ethnic, or sexual grounds. That such discrimination is undemocratic no longer needs to be stressed. It is universally understood. One may argue that the state should respect free choice, and not force people of different backgrounds and interests to live together if they do not wish to. But in order that the principle of equal opportunity may prevail, false barriers in housing, employment, education, medical treatment, and recreational facilities must be broken down. As I have stressed, the chief method of change should be voluntary and persuasive. I would in principle prefer, for example, voluntary to compulsory busing to achieve racial balance. Where constitutional liberties are denied, however, the courts must intervene to guarantee individual rights and equal opportunity.

Many political democracies, as in Latin America or Europe, may be purely formal. In a closed society, there are strong class lines and a hierarchy, based upon wealth, birth, or tradition, making it virtually impossible for one from a lower station in society to break through. An open society would allow full mobility. It would, as far as possible, break down class lines, and thus make interaction, intermarriage, and fraternization possible. In England and France, old class societies, such mobility has been difficult. In the United States and the Soviet Union less so.

We are often told that the United States is a class society; hence, its bourgeois democracy is deceptive. What is the meaning of "class"? The 19th-century Marxist definition does not seem strictly applicable to the current scene. In an advanced agricultural technology less than six per cent of the population are now needed on the farms. Hence, the peasantry which once made up a significant part of society has virtually disappeared. The percentage of industrial workers engaged in production is also becoming a smaller part of the labor force; skilled labor is replacing unskilled; the expert technician is assuming a more important role; the number of people in service occupations, in the professions, and in governmental service is growing significantly and is now greater than those in production.

The increasing tendency of corporations to get larger—large-scale industries and trusts prevail in socialist as well as capitalist societies —is harmful to decentralization and democracy. In the United States, where there is a separation between ownership and management, the capitalists alone do not run industry. Consequently, the over-simplified model of the proletarian class on one side of the barricades and the capitalist class on the other is a romantic fiction that Marxists attempt to keep alive, but that has little applicability to contemporary conditions. Recently some Marxists have lumped students and blacks into the proletarian class in an effort to increase its size, but this destroys the classical model, for the basis of the distinction here is age and race rather than economic interest.

Is class based upon property? Two-thirds of American families own their own homes, and large numbers own stocks or bonds. Is class based upon earnings from interest, rent, dividends? Virtually everyone draws earnings from interest in savings accounts; many people earn money from rent. Millions of workers and retired people own insurance annuities or have retirement plans, drawing dividends and capital gains. One can not deny the maldistribution of wealth and other inequities in capitalist society, but these do not follow strict class lines. Presumably progressive taxation and other feasible kinds of adjustment could rectify these inequities.

The notion of class makes most sense not simply as an economic term, but in its reference to the existence of a power structure, and to distinctions in power and responsibility based upon role and function. There is a power elite that makes decisions and directs the affairs of institutions. But socialist societies have discovered that they too need bureaucrats to direct the large-scale state trusts, industries, and communes, much like the managers in so-called capitalist societies. Given this reality there is a need to democratize the power structure and to see that large institutions come under effective democratic political control. But there is also a need to change the character and selection of elites within these institutions. Anti-democratic tendencies in elites can only be modified where the principles of liberty and equality operate. To have elites is not in itself wicked. It is hard to see how a complex modern society can exist without them. What is important is that membership in an elite group be based upon proven merit and talent, that it be made responsive to public needs, and that it not be overladen with privileges and rights that are unavailable to others.

ORGANIZATIONAL DEMOCRACY

It is unfortunate that, in the history of political theory, many democrats have concentrated upon political or social democracy in the government and state as if these were the only areas where democracy might be applied. A large and significant struggle has been waged in which the people have attempted to extract concessions from authoritarian governments, and in which the principles of liberty and equality have been recognized by the state. But the democratic ideal will not be fulfilled without being extended to other institutions.

Thus, the new democratic frontier is to be found in a variety of organizations, associations, and institutions within society. It is often not the state or the government that is the oppressive instrument which exposes the individual to alienating forces, but rather the church, the economy, the school, the family. Such organizations as General Motors, I.T.T., the Mormon Church, McGraw-Hill, the AFL-CIO, the University of California, are complex, imperial structures. They have become in some instances larger than many national governments or states. We have been aware of this serious development for some time. Berle and Means pointed out back in the 'thirties the danger of the growth of the corporation, the concentration of economic power in a limited number of hands, the divorce between ownership and control. But we have since become aware that it is not simply the growth of economic corporations that is the characteristic of our society (or of other complex industrial societies), but the growth of organizations in general—even though other organizations have been influenced by the corporate model: labor unions, farmers' groups, cooperatives, political parties, government bureaus, colleges and universities, hospitals, prisons, churches, television networks, newspaper chains, publishing houses, associations, clubs of all sorts. The organizational growth trend is not necessarily toward monopoly, but oligopoly—i.e., a limited number of large organizations dominating a field.

The result of this concentration is that we are faced with a new dilemma which did not exist for liberal democrats in the nineteenth century or even in the early part of the twentieth: the displacement of personality by "organizality" and the surrender of the individual to the organization. What is clear is that our theories of ethical duty and responsibility have failed to diagnose the condition of contemporary man or to provide adequate proposals for its solution. Indeed, one of the reasons why the individual today frequently feels powerless to affect decision-making processes in his society is that decisions emanate from organizations, not individuals. The entrepreneur of Adam Smith's day, the writer or free thinker of John Stuart Mill's day, are rapidly being replaced by the corporate organization, the publishing firm, or the multiversity. If we analyze the term "responsibility," we find that if viewed in terms of the individual it has lost much of its meaning, for to say that someone ought to do something implies that he has the power to act and to effect change. The point is that individuals by themselves have been shorn of power. Hence responsibility is organizational insofar as power and capacity are organizational.

Mankind has for centuries had huge organizations: the Roman Empire, the Catholic Church, among others. But with the vast increase of population and the economic development of society, the tendency toward organization—vast and impersonal—has increased. Organization is one of the basic keys to human progress. It is founded on the discovery that specialization and the division of labor are the keys to productivity and efficiency. The organized factory system and mass production made possible rapid industrialization. Organizations have also made possible large systems of distribution and communication, mass education, teams for scientific research, efficient armies, and the fulfillment of many other social purposes. The organizational revolution is an essential part of the technological revolution.

PARTICIPATORY DEMOCRACY

From the standpoint of democracy, it is important that organizations be reformed and the democratic ethos extended to them. What we need is to develop an "organizational bill of rights," an emancipation proclamation by means of which we can build a plurality of democratic organizations. What should be done is always relative, but some general observations can nonetheless be made.

We have examined the position of the anarchist who demands that large organizations be abolished: "Man is born free but is everywhere in organizations." Hence to liberate human beings we must destroy organizations. It is clear that this proposal is sheer utopianism; modern life is so complex that without some organizational structures there would be a breakdown of civilized life. There are too many services and functions to be performed which only the ordering of energies can accomplish. It is conceivable that with a vast increase of automation the necessity for organizations may be lessened; but their withering away at this stage of development is not feasible.

There is also the recommendation of Marxists that organizations, particularly economic corporations, be nationalized and placed under state control. This proposal has had an allure for liberals who look to the government as a countervailing power, in a position to restrict the power of monopoly formations, but there is no guarantee that still another superbureaucracy will correct the defects of an organizational society, or that it will not bring in its wake the still more terrible effects of a totalitarian society. The Soviet Union is an organizational society, but it has hardly solved the problem of the suppressed individual. A society in which there is a plurality of organizations guarantees a higher measure of freedom for the individual than one in which the state dominates organizations. The panacea of central government planning of organizational life must be seriously questioned. But this does not preclude, and indeed one may argue for, government regulation of organizations and indeed governmental ownership of a limited number (a mixed economy). The Securities and Exchange Commission, Federal Communication Commission, National Labor Relations Board, or Congressional investigations of industry, illustrate the therapeutic role that government can play by regulating rather than by outright control; and partial nationalization, as of the railroads and banks in Europe, or the TVA in the United States, shows the important stimulus that this can have on the economy.

There are other avenues of reform beyond complete nationalization. The legal system and the courts can be enlisted to guarantee due process within institutions, and there is the power of public opinion and of moral suasion. All organizations—business, labor, education, the churches, and private associations—must be constantly examined publicly, for many large organizations have become quasi-legal and in some sense public properties. There is a method of control, however ineffective it sometimes is, that can be exerted by the clientele of the corporate organizations: Consumers can protest by refusing to buy products, and by complaining to sponsors of the mass media; voters can make known their objections to their Congressmen, students can protest bad teaching and bad administration, and parishioners can refuse to attend churches. It is the responsibility of the organization to fulfill its service functions, and where it distorts the process the users have a right to insist that it cease and desist, and to demand quality of performance. There is a growing awareness of this power in our consumer unions and student cooperatives, in the professional associations and groups which set proper standards for organizations (American Association of University Professors, American Bar Association, American Civil Liberties Union, etc.); and we can create new organizations to combat nondemocratic organizations.

It is also important that public members concerned with the public interest be appointed to Boards of Directors. Here the consumer interest needs to be respected and the needs of the community for ecological and environmental concern. In this, it seems to me, lies the importance of Naderism as a movement. Perhaps we need to extend stockholder ownership of the corporations extensively and make the workers the real owners of their own industries. The point is, we need to be open to creative, alternative methods of developing democracy in all large organizations, particularly in economic institutions.

I do not believe, however, that these modes of reform by themselves are sufficient. They do not fully appreciate the centrality of the humanistic ethical principle which finds individuality a positive good and which seeks to rescue the individual from the forces that negate him. In the light of this principle, what we need to do is to reform and transform organizations by the men in the organizations themselves.

There are various types of government within organization: monarchic rule by family inheritance, autocratic tryanny, oligarchical rule by an elite (the dominant mode in our corporate and financial trusts), or rule by democracy. It is the democratic process within the organization that we should defend. It is there that our true hope rests.

Some insist that an organization requires an administrative structure if it is to be efficient, that democracy will not work. It is of course clear that in their need for leaders organizations cannot avoid hierarchical structures; an elite is bound to develop to some extent. The same thing is inevitably true in the political field. The matters here at issue are rather the procedures employed in selecting leaders, in changing elites, and in making hierarchies sensitive to criticism. The democrat may argue that representative government is essential even in organizations (which are too complex for town-hall-meeting governments), that the leaders should in some sense represent all members of an organization, that organization personnel have some stake in their selection, and that rule should not be imposed from above.

Unfortunately directors of large corporations often represent self-perpetuating oligarchies, they are rarely elected by the stockholders, or by the workers and foremen in the plants. It is regrettable as well that many officials of labor unions establish closed dynasties which are very difficult to break, and that ecclesiastical hierarchies still dominate many of the churches. Many of our educational institutions have introduced some measure of democratic participation by faculties and students, but it is clear that the real power of most institutions of higher learning still lies with absentee Boards of Trustees (in many cases self-appointed), and that the officials they elect to carry out their policies are more often responsive to them than to the people within their organizations.

What I am stressing is the need to respect participation at all levels in the decision-making process. We need decentralization of our organizational structures so that decisions may also be made on the lower rungs. Above all, what we need is the principle of *freedom of dissent* and the *right of opposition* within the organization itself. At times this may even mean the right of *corporate disobedience*. If there are no legal mechanisms for a change in policies or for the redress of grievances, one has a right to disobey—within the limits of prudence and balance—in accordance with, not in violation of, civil laws. Corporate organizations all too rarely tolerate or respect disagreements, all too rarely admit honest differences of opinion (outside of the elite). They prefer to impose sanctions and penalties upon those who resist the organizational system and who dissent from policies—cutting off increments and promotions, reducing salaries, or ultimately ordering expulsions. The counter methods available to workers—the picket line, the slowdown, the strike, resignation, accepting another position—have shown how sharp a cutting edge there is in mobility. The point is, a person has a right to continue to be part of an organized group to which he has devoted his time and energy even if he dissents from or disobeys its policy directives.

Contemporary American society is often said to be quasi-competitive; the real competition exists more among organizations than individuals. To compete, we are told, an organization must be efficient; hence the argument for administrative coercion. But the fear of coercion should not be the sole determinant of an employee's motivation. There are other subtle factors, among them confidence in the administration and belief that what one is doing is worthwhile.

We need to develop pluralistic democracies in organizations which would encourage responsible individuals to speak out against malpractices and to defend what they hold to be worthwhile without fear of reprisals. Of course private industries, even if they are controlled by those who work within them, may continue to be self-interested and to that extent perhaps against the public good.

COMPETENCE AND THE LIMITS OF PARTICIPATION

As I have said earlier in regard to the principles of liberty and equality, general principles are guides for policy and action, to be tested by their consequences and in pragmatic terms. Participatory democracy, though a general principle that I defend, must be applied in context if it is to be meaningful. Individual participation must of course be related to the functions of the particular organization.

Participatory democracy in an army, for example, has its uses up to a point, but it also obviously has its limitations. If a nation wants to win a war, a certain degree of discipline must be enforced and military orders and regulations obeyed, else chaos will result, and an army will become a mob.

The German General Staff created in the Wehrmacht an army of unquestioning obedience to orders; but it might be argued, in defense of participatory democracy, that if an army's loyalty were based upon intelligent commitment and participation rather than fear, it would contribute to morale and efficiency; that an obedient mass is no substitute for individual initiative, intelligence, and skill; that the stupidities and mistakes of an "infallible" officer class may be unmasked by the practical wisdom of noncommissioned officers and enlisted men; and that a citizens' militia in a democracy is to be preferred to sole dependence upon a professional army cadre. The democratization of the ranks may thus contribute to the performance of the chief function of the military organization. Yet we all recognize that some limitation on democracy is necessary as long as nation-states and armies exist. One cannot debate whether to go into battle when an opposing army menaces.

There are comparable advantages in the democratization of prisons and other penal institutions but within obvious limits. A prison where inmates can participate to some degree in decisions affecting their welfare, where individuality is not destroyed by constraint, and where prisoners are able to develop potentialities, is bound to be able to rehabilitate them better than one run by compulsion and command. Yet if incarceration is deemed necessary, participatory democracy has its limitations when order must be imposed. It is obvious that each institution must be democratized in a specifically characteristic way.

One might argue, for example, that hospital patients should be consulted concerning treatment and care, food and fees and have the final say as to whether they want to be treated; but doctors and nurses are usually better able on the basis of knowledge and skill than patients to evaluate the wisdom of a course of treatment.

The most frequent confusion in the relationship of participatory democracy to competence may be seen in the universities, which are for the most part hierarchial organizations made up of three estates:

administration, faculty, and students. From one side comes the demand that faculty participate in important policy decisions and wrest power from administrations. The imposition by Boards of Regents and Trustees of administrative officials—often success-achievers—upon faculty, and the view that professors are "employees," primarily passive and security-oriented, are archaic. As a result faculty members often become ambivalent toward their universities. But what after all is a top-flight university, if it is not its faculty? Who should run the university, if not the faculty? The overemphasis upon bureaucracy is to be deplored; the same degree of centralization does not exist in comparable European institutions. Administrators, where necessary, should be elected by the faculty, serve as their representatives, with powers only as delegated by faculty. The argument of competence or special qualifications does not apply here; one may argue that administrators are no more competent than the faculty, probably less so.

From still another quarter comes the demand that students should participate in all decisions and share power equally with the faculty and the administration. The student often finds the multiversity remote from his interests, hierarchical, conservative, and bureaucratic. From his point of view the faculty often represents an elite whose first commitment is to narrow specialization. The student is considered an unimportant element within the knowledge factory. No wonder that students often have felt alienated, like plastic-wrapped consumer products, standardized, replaceable, largely irrelevant. The archaic university stands in relation to its students as a parent does, and it can control their conduct to virtually the same extent that parents can. In many universities the student is an outsider whose chief virtue is submission to authority. Students must knuckle under to rules and regulations; those who are "difficult" may be disciplined by suspension or expulsion.

The arguments in favor of granting some measure of personal involvement to students are numerous. An excellent university should not be organized along corporate authoritarian lines, but to activate the creative potential in both students and faculty. The two estates should share in the common enterprise of learning and research and thus become a community of scholars in the full sense. What better way for students to learn if not by personal identification with the process of education? What better way to be stimulated toward goals than by participating in creating them? Students are entitled to be treated as adults and individuals; and they should join with professors in the noble effort of developing the university.

Yet, after all is said, the university is a peculiar kind of organization; it is by its nature hierarchical, though this (in theory at least) is based not upon birth, class, or wealth, but upon scholarly attainment. In most universities of quality there are careful processes of selection and standards of tenure; in order to be appointed a faculty member, to be promoted and receive the emoluments required, one must demonstrate qualifications in education, and experience. Tenure, an essential component in all great universities, protects the academic freedom of the professor, *Lehrfreiheit,* without fear of censorship or reprisal, and it assures promotion with the highest standards of excellence. There is always the danger that an entrenched oligarchy of senior professors will attempt to keep out new ideas and fresh blood. Junior faculty need safeguards against prejudicial treatment, and they need a method for redress of grievances.

Freedom and tenure are the essential principles upon which a university committed to the free pursuit of knowledge is based. If the students' right to learn cannot be questioned, however, it does not qualify them for the rights and privileges which faculty members of demonstrated competence possess: to teach and to further research.

Students should be given the opportunity to participate, but not to control academic policies. They are not qualified to teach higher mathematics or advanced philosophy, nor can they be responsible for the curriculum. They cannot make up or grade examinations, or set standards for the granting of degrees. They are not competent to judge the quality of a professor's research, though they may judge his teaching to some extent. Learning is the primary responsibility of the student, teaching and research the primary responsibilities of the faculty, and the functions should not be confused. Besides competence in a field of specialization, there are certain professional standards which faculty members possess, as doctors and lawyers do. It is absurd to expect medical or law students to qualify as doctors or lawyers before they have graduated or passed the bar exams but they should be given every opportunity to learn by doing, and to contribute to the educational process. It would be similarly absurd to expect students to qualify as professional educators. The policy of allowing each vote—of student and faculty member—to count for one is made even more untenable by the fact that students are apt to be transient whereas educators have a lifetime involvement in education.

There are other dangers. Devotees of an ethical principle may be so carried away by its virtues that they fail to make distinctions. Participation does not mean politicizing the university. It does not mean that the purposes of the university can be dominated by political pressure groups. It does not mean that vocal minorities, or *a fortiori* suppressive majorities, can intimidate the community of scholarship. It does not mean that force can be used to coerce faculties. It does mean that a university is a place for reason and moderation, for responsible criticism and the free market of ideas, committed to the involvement of students, faculty, and administrators in the educational process.

The crucial question often asked is: if students and faculty share in the common task of education, which decisions are to be made by students and which by faculty? It is clear that students should be primarily concerned with those standards which concern their behavior and moral choices. *In loco parentis* is no longer justifiable. The private lives and social activities of students are their own business, including what they do off and on campuses, within the bounds of civil law.

They should have the freedom to invite speakers to campus, to organize groups, to publish newspapers and magazines. They should have the full protection of those freedoms which are the right of all other citizens in a democracy, all consistent with the idea of an open campus. Students should be permitted to grade their professors as a contribution to the improvement of university teaching; they should assist in selecting scholars in residence or visiting professors, within the limits of the budget; and permitted to suggest new courses and programs. They should be consulted about university facilities, the library, bookstore, cafeteria, transportation, fees, and tuition—they should be involved in all matters which concern their welfare directly.

Certain decisions should be left to the faculty, among them standards for admission and graduation, grading of student performance, curricular content and subject matter of courses, the goals of the university, the character of faculty or university-sponsored research, faculty appointments, promotions, and tenure, the free expression of ideas. These prerogatives appropriately follow from their professional competence.

There are decisions which concern both students and faculty. They should always maintain continuous dialogue on a number of issues: facilities which the faculty also use, such as the library, bookstore, and cafeteria, the university calendar, the initiation of new programs, new services, long-range goals, and so on. There are many creative methods by which cooperative ventures may be enacted: a university-wide senate in which the faculty is predominant, should contain student representation; student participation in committees—perhaps not in all but in those which concern student affairs and policy directly; open discussion of issues by faculty and students in the classroom, in forums and debates, in publications, and so on. The life blood of a university is one in which there is a free give and take on all sides.

Participatory democracy in those institutions where competence and knowledge are basic does not entail egalitarianism or unbridled liberty. To paraphrase Aristotle, it involves a form of proportional equality, relative to the competence of the participants, which must not be indiscriminately applied. Organizations may claim specialized competence as a basis for excluding personnel from decision-making. Such exclusion would be fraudulent in many cases; it may, as we have seen, be meaningful in the university, but only insofar as it achieves the furtherance of learning.

Participatory democracy should allow competence to emerge; it provides the best opportunities for commitment and talent. It does not deny leadership, or the emergence of elites of demonstrated merit, but seeks to make them representative. The premise of the democratic value system is that "he who wears the shoe best knows where it pinches." The most reliable way to direct an organization is to give the people in it a chance to contribute to its functioning.

Society has presented us with the new and complex phenomenon of large-scale organizalities ready to suffocate the individual. We need to reawaken the sense of democratic community within organizations. There are dimensions of responsibility that can only be expressed by the individual in terms of his hopes and ideals, which cannot be relinquished to any organization. Our humanist concern is based upon a concern for this individual freedom.

To repeat, the institutions of society are tested by whether or not they help individuals to express their talents and contribute to the common good. If so, they will help to resolve the problem of alienation in the postmodern world.

Part Three / Prospects for the Future

IX / A Global Consciousness

INTRODUCTION

Thus far we have been dealing with questions that concern the individual: We have asked, What is the fullness of life? We have been concerned with questions of the just society: How do the principles of libertarianism, tolerance, equal rights, and participatory democracy apply? Our concern has been to meet the possibility that contemporary life may be empty and without meaning for us. But the problem of alienation and the present dilemma of man are of wider scope and have deeper impact. Any adequate treatment of the crisis of contemporary man must consider the question in its global dimensions.

The problem cannot be resolved by way of the comparatively simpler considerations of the individuals or of a particular society. It is transnational in character. A reflective person who is morally concerned must at some point extend his range of interest to the

185

wider community of man. One cannot help but recognize the claims that all men now have on every man.

There are mammoth problems for the entire human race: the conflicts between national states, the disparities between the have and have-not nations, poverty and deprivation, overpopulation, misuses of world resources, industrial pollution, technological destruction, the dangers and promises of new forms of technology. Political leaders who have been attempting to deal with such problems on a national level have been forced increasingly to recognize their universality. Government planners are confronted daily with unassailable evidence, in working out economic or foreign policies, that it cannot be done fruitfully unless and until the world develops a global policy with some moral guidelines for the future. Any humanism worthy of the name must address itself to the larger existential situation of the human race, difficult as that may be. If it is a complex matter to deal with any of the problems of one society, the complexities on the international scale are compounded immeasurably. There is no need to spell out further homilies on the concept of one world. Thinking people have so widely understood the growing interdependence of the continents in this century that it has become a truism. What is not sufficiently widely recognized, however, is the need for global solutions. We need to develop, now, a plan of what a peaceful and prosperous world might be like. Any hope for a better future must be for mankind as a whole. In this connection, there are three looming problems that I wish to focus upon.

A WORLD ORDER

The Problem

By means of a slow evolutionary process, small social units, such as the tribe or city-state, have grown in territory and population into what we now call nation-states. There are now over 140 sovereign nations in the world; each has mastery over a defined territory, with a group of people who share traditions and values, a common linguistic heritage, and a way of life. In each national group there exist an economic system and a political order, with codes of law defining conduct and behavior within the territorial confines.

Governments may change, different economic systems may be instituted, but the nation-state as an identifiable entity persists. Accordingly, the concept of sovereignty designates the power of the nation-state as constant, though political and economic structures change. Sovereignty applies to various kinds of states: democratic, oligarchical, aristocratic, totalitarian, hereditary, or republican. The concept of sovereignty, if demythologized and divorced from metaphysical overtones, implies that there is a basic source of authority in a nation-state, even though there is always a contest for control and the center of power may be divided between competing groups. I have already stated my judgment that a democratic political system and majority rule best express the sovereign will of a society, entail fewest risks, and fulfill the needs of the greatest number of people.

The emergence of centralized political control of a territorial jurisdiction made an important contribution to the evolution of society. The monarchs of Western Europe battled with lesser nobles for hegemony; new territories were subjected by invasion to the control of a centralized sovereign. By unifying disparate elements national states made possible a new structure of order, and by establishing relative conditions of peace and tranquility, banishing fear, and ensuring safety, enabled the arts of modern civilization to develop. Later, the sovereign state was entrusted with the task not only of providing defense and protection, but of securing the welfare of the people. It was able to tax for the common good and to provide for economic, educational, and cultural development.

In time, the ideal of nationhood emerged and out of that grew a sense of nationality. As individuals identified themselves as German, English or Argentinian, patriotism became a powerful bond for people within an area. As people within a state married, shared a common heritage and folklore, and as their means of communication began to improve, they became increasingly conscious of their national identity; ties were reinforced by the kinship and consanguinity of a common genetic stock. This historical development had a double effect: While it contributed to a wider extension of human relationships within the nation, it also in time led to nationalism and to a feeling of separation from those who lived in other nation-states and participated in other linguistic and cultural traditions.

Nationalism has been a powerful unifying symbol, fulfilling a quasi-religious function in human experience. *Pro patria* largely replaced *pro ecclesia* as a source of devotion and dedication. If men in early times were willing to die for God and Church, they would now sacrifice themselves more resolutely for country. Patriotism became the highest moral commitment of the young who went off to the wars, and the flag and other symbols of national entity and historic destiny were used to evoke a religion of civic piety.

In many contexts nationalism is still progressive. It gives a sense of purpose to life by providing a basis for attempts to liberate a common group of people from foreign domination. Ethnic, cultural, and racial minorities hunger for national identity, self-determination, autonomy, and, often unwilling to be assimilated, they demand independence from larger political units: the Czechs and Hungarians in central Europe, Biafrans in Nigeria, Bangladesh in East Pakistan, Irish Catholics in Northern Ireland, Ukrainians in the Soviet Union, French in Canada. Nationalism also provides a rallying cry against exploitation by colonial powers; the underdeveloped countries of the Third World, especially the Vietnamese, graphically demonstrate this. Nationalism thus forges a sense of identity and purpose and an ideal of emancipation.

But the concept of sovereignty and the ideal of nationalism have had unsettling consequences; the world has been transformed into a jungle of competing states, and the result is too often war and destruction. We are today witnessing a renaissance of tribalism—ethnic calls for liberation from oppressive groups splinter the world even more, precipitating tension and sometimes warfare. In modern Yugoslavia, for example, there are at least six national groups (Serbs, Croats, Slovenes, Montenegrins, and others) and the competitive distinctions among them jeopardize the unity of the country. In a sense, the proliferation of nation-states that could ensue is retrogressive, for it increases conflict. With the breakdown of former colonial empires, the pluralistic system of competing states that has emerged may take us further from the possibility of world government than before. Nationalism is both liberating and reactionary, since our pressing global need is to transcend such tribal loyalties and to aspire toward the wider community of all humanity.

Such writers as Robert Ardrey and Konrad Lorenz believe that the territorial imperative is instinctive and that war is an expression of the deepest biological urgings of man and other species. Whether or not they are right, it is at least the case that the existence of separate tribal groups and nation-states, each a law unto itself, has exacerbated the conditions for strife, and with the development of ever more sophisticated instruments of warfare, caused terrible slaughter. In the name of the nation, men have been willing to commit heinous crimes against those of their fellow human beings whom they do not consider equals.

Without a system of world law, it is difficult to restrain those who control power from using it for selfish reasons and misusing it against those with whom they disagree, within or without their borders. National power has fallen under the capricious will of tyrants and despots, self-righteous rulers interested in aggrandizement and domination. Modern man is cursed with the state, a hazardous political-economic-social entity, and faced with the continuous possibility of its being used to threaten him with violence.

In earlier epochs, when communication and transportation were more limited, nations the size of Spain or France were relatively circumscribed and nation-states so limited in size and jurisdiction made some sense, for it was difficult to manage countries so large that outlying provinces were inaccessible. No longer. Communication is virtually instantaneous throughout the world and travel relatively easy. Immigration and emigration, extensive economic trade and cultural contacts, are essential parts of the common life of mankind. Corporations, cartels, and trusts conduct business on a global scale. Science, art, poetry, music, philosophy, and religion are international in scope as well; the diaspora of artists, scientists, intellectuals, enables them to feel at home in almost any part of the world. For the first time in the history of mankind there are no cultural groups that are able to thrive in privacy independent of others. Human history is no longer Western or Asian, primitive or advanced. We are all part of an increasingly global culture. The nation-state which seeks to circumscribe culture is now an anachronism.

Since World War II virtually all the major powers have gone to war and committed atrocities in the name of their so-called vital national interests. If Germany, Japan and Italy committed unspeakable acts in World War II, others have followed, if on a lesser scale: France in Algeria, Russia in Hungary and Czechoslovakia, China in

Korea, the United States in Vietnam, Britain and France in Suez, Israel and Egypt, Ireland and Britain, Russia and China along their borders, India and Pakistan, and so on. Most of the attempts to reach solutions by means of partition have caused additional problems: North and South Vietnam, North and South Korea, East and West Berlin, East and West Pakistan, etc. Nationalism is the virulent disease which must be eliminated if we are to survive.

The overriding political need today is to develop some form of democratic world order, in which there is some degree of centralized power and authority, a new source of sovereignty stronger than any of the separate sovereignties that comprise it. The purpose of such a transnational state would be to provide for common defense, to reduce conflict, and contribute to the economic and cultural enrichment of the entire human race.

It is a pity that the dream of world government is not more vivid today, that the youth particularly are not inspired by its appeal. What better way is there to fulfill the truly religious hunger for meaning and commitment than by pursuing the ideal of world community? With "the death of God" and the obsolescence of nationalism, the next move should be toward the building of one world. Many are enraptured by Marxist socialism. No world government without it, they say. But world government is an ideal that desperately needs a combined constituency—now.

One encouraging development here is a growing world-wide disillusionment with patriotism. Widespread civil disobedience and draft evasion were of course active in the United States during the Vietnam war. There is a similar debunking of chauvinism in many countries of the world, a revulsion against the old nationalistic symbols at least in the developed nations—Germany, Sweden, France, Denmark, and Britain, for example—if not in the underdeveloped nations, where nationalism can still play a progressive role. That the young are cynical about the heroic military virtues is a hopeful sign. The next step must be the development of a world conscience dedicated to bringing about a genuine world community. One individual quite naturally feels ineffectual in confronting world problems; what, he asks, can *I* do for the whole of humanity? But the Peace Corps, for example, has dramatized the inspiring phenomenon of putting idealisms into action. Now we critically need to develop a sense of the high importance, the moral urgency of world community.

A World Community

World government would not be like either the League of Nations or the United Nations; for both of these organizations have been composed of sovereign nation-states that entered into an international compact for reasons of self-interest. To achieve a genuine world community, nation-states would have to relinquish some of their independence by giving sovereignty to a world body that would transcend nations. It would not be at the beck and call of the member states, but an independent entity, with political, legal and economic power of its own greater, as I have stressed, than that of any of its members.

There are at least five basic developments necessary if we are to achieve genuine world order:

(1)   We must work toward the development of a consensus, common values, and a common cultural tradition. The business of the world has not usually been determined by moral considerations. The highest principle should be that which furthers the welfare of mankind collectively.

(2)   Accordingly, we must work toward a central political sovereignty which would control a preponderance of the world's coercive power and, thus equipped, could provide for the common defense. This must of course be preceded by some degree of disarmament among the nations. In a world order one nation's use of violence to impose its will upon another is rendered impossible. But such an order is possible only with a world police force more powerful than any of the nations' forces.

The world is not, at present, in a state of anarchy. There are *de facto* equilibrating systems. The balance of power principle is still operative; there are mutual security arrangements, regional groupings, the balance of nuclear terror. Even enemies recognize common self-interests and have some understanding of limits and constraints. The United States and the Soviet Union, for example, apparently wish to contain and localize small wars that do not involve their vital interests. These interests tend to restrain large-scale war but the question is whether they provide adequate safeguards. Those who believe in world government maintain that the present system is not adequate and will have to be replaced by a more effective machinery of universal collective security.

(3)   A political world order must of course be capable of enacting laws and enforcing them. The rule of law is a cardinal foundation of civilization. Laws grow out of common practice and consent, but as they must be legislatively enacted, judicially interpreted, and executively applied, we need a world legislature, a world judiciary and a world executive, each empowered to carry out such indispensable functions.

(4)   A world body should possess some economic power and be capable of imposing taxes upon the wealthy nations in order to finance development of the poorer nations. We can no longer depend upon grants of aid by major powers in accordance with their own narrow interests. The United Nations now has a global plan for development but it is far too limited. As a first step, wealthy nations should be taxed a minimum of 1 per cent of their gross national product. And it should be increased gradually up to at least 7 per cent —what is presently being spent on arms budgets in the United States and the Soviet Union. This means that the U.S.A. eventually would alone contribute at least 90 billions of its resources per year to world development.

(5)   World government must inevitably encourage a maximum of educational and social opportunity and development, free access across frontiers, and the greatest degree of cultural contact. The member peoples would grow enormously in awareness, in tolerance, and in good will through appreciation of the cultural traditions and achievements of other areas of the world.

As I see it, the world government must be democratic, cultivating, in fact inspiring, decentralized autonomy and freedom. Nation-states, races, and ethnic groups need not disappear; though with intercommunication and intermarriage their differences would naturally become less important, their traditions should not be abolished but rather encouraged to play a role in the context of world community.

A federal transnational system would allow for both unity and diversity, with various political, social, and economic systems operating within it. Advanced societies may be democratic; less developed ones may adopt other forms of government. The point is, a world order need not impose a uniform system on all states, its purpose would be to represent the people of the world collectively rather than as citizens whose interests always correspond to those of their separate and competing nation-states.

How to Bring World Government About

A cause for much despair among world federalists is the fact that world government has been so slow in developing. Some have trusted in the evolutionary process, hoping that in time world-wide institutions would develop. Some wished to work within the League of Nations; others now work within the United Nations, believing that it will evolve into the instrumentality of world government. But there is room for skepticism; the UN is a conglomerate of nations, not peoples, and its powers are limited. The way to bring about genuine world government is by fundamental revision of the Charter of the UN to minimize the role of the Security Council and nullify the veto power; it would bring in all states now outside the UN and make population the arbiter of decision-making in the Assembly. Perhaps both a Senate and an Assembly would best fulfill the need for fair representation. Today, little Bhutan's vote is equal to that of the United States, China, the USSR. Perhaps states with populations over 200 million should have the same number of votes and smaller states fewer votes, commensurate in some way with population. At any rate, some system of proportional representation would seem to be fairer.

How can such fundamental reform be effected? Will the nation-states of the world recognize that it is in their self-interest to relinquish sovereignty to a world body? Will the threats of overpopulation, waste, resource depletion, economic chaos, nuclear or chemical-biological warfare, impel them to do so? They can arrive at that juncture only if a consensus develops among the world's peoples and if the ideal of the unity of mankind arouses both rational commitment and emotional support. Nation-states, large and small, today can defy the resolutions of the UN because no effective centralized force exists to carry out decisions of the Security Council, Assembly, or Secretary-General; there is no recognized legislature, judiciary, or instrumentality for enforcement; there is no deep sense of moral authority.

The need for world government is too important a matter to be left to the dilly-dallying of politicians, ambassadors, presidents, or premiers. In many respects the situation is far worse than it was a decade or two ago, for independent nation-states have proliferated, and they are still beyond the limitations or sanctions of higher authority in questions concerning their vital national aspirations. World government cannot wait for the United Nations to evolve into a world governmental system; as a union of independent nation-states, it may never do so.

It is therefore essential that world opinion recognize the need for, and insist upon, thoroughgoing charter revision. If this kind of pressure cannot accomplish the task, then perhaps it should be entrusted to nonpolitical leaders—in the arts and sciences, religion, labor, and business. It may be that we need a new world constitutional convention in which the peoples of the world can transcend national jurisdictions and move across frontiers. We need to make world citizenship a reality. One step forward would be for countries now willing to renounce sovereignty to do so by joining a world federation; and we should encourage regional and other forms of federation, as in the Common Market and the commonwealth countries. If world government cannot be achieved within the UN—and we should leave no avenue unexplored—then it should be achieved outside it. Massive effort is needed in every possible direction.

For the United States the long-term tragedy of the Vietnam War was not simply that it wasted human resources, led to brutal slaughter, or split the nation apart in controversy, but that it deflected what should have been the chief aim of foreign policy: the building of world government. Liberals, radicals, leftists, and socialists, in their just concern with ending the war in Vietnam—only one aspect of the global scene—did not sufficiently concentrate on the overriding need to construct institutions for a world order. It is only when such institutions come into being that some kind of world disarmament will occur and international tensions be reduced, and some transfer of weapon systems from nation-states to a transnational police force be effected. Only then can the enormous sums expended on armaments be turned to urgent peaceful purposes.

Although, as I have said, the aim of world government should first be collective security, it should also be concerned with economic, cultural, educational and social cooperation—the area in which the UN has made its most significant contribution, though on a scale far too small. The decision whether to implement the Universal Declaration of Human Rights should no longer be entrusted exclusively to individual states. The fact that the West Pakistan army could suppress human rights within Pakistan is a matter of world concern, as is the policy of apartheid in South Africa, the plight of political prisoners in Greece or Cuba, or the suppression of minorities and intellectuals in the Soviet Union. We must not only be concerned about maintaining peace and security between states, but must try to ensure the protection of the individual's rights within them. World government should guarantee individual freedom and equality in all parts of the globe.

A world community in which the rule of law and international cooperation prevails, however, will not necessarily end political and social conflicts between peoples. New dangers will no doubt arise: the possibility of a world dictatorship, of civil rather than national wars, of the domination of one area by another, the oppression of cultural movements, the suppression of civil liberties, among others. One cannot foretell the future but it is certain that new challenges will emerge. Utopia is an ideal, and world government will not ensure utopia but, given the intense problems posed by the existence of separate nation-states and the need for global cooperation, it is clear that some system of world government is critically necessary.

WORLD ECONOMIC DEVELOPMENT

Among the chief obstacles at present are the intense animosities engendered by an ideological-religious Marxism and the antagonisms, allegedly inevitable, between the socialist and capitalist systems. Marxists avow belief in the *Internationale*—the ideal of one world in which the workers and peasants control and share equally in the products of society. The chief obstacle to world order, it is alleged,

is capitalism, particularly in its imperialist phase. The existence of
international trusts and cartels, say the Marxists, makes a world
order impossible, for the tentacles of capitalist power are everywhere,
reaching out into and exploiting backward areas. U.S. economic
interests interlace the globe—importing tin from Bolivia, copper
from Chile, tungsten from the Congo, oil from the Middle East, and
seeking markets to export manufactured goods and capital. Today
Japanese, German, French, British, and Dutch capital competes with
American industry for control of world markets. How can there be
a genuine world order, they ask, while the wealthy states still exploit
the poorer, underdeveloped areas?

It should now be clear that the orthodox Marxist explanation is
oversimplified. Imperialism and colonialism are not the preserve
only of the capitalist or quasi-capitalist societies; socialist and communist states behave in similar ways in regard to their client states.
The Soviet Union dominates client states in Eastern Europe: Czechoslovakia, Poland, and Hungary dare not break away from Soviet
hegemony; Yugoslavia and Rumania tread dangerous ground; and
China indicts the Soviet Union continuously as an imperialist power
seeking to dominate her. The international power and influence of
the Soviet Union have grown into the vacuum left by departing
capitalist colonial powers in the Middle East, on the continents of
Africa and Asia, and in Latin America. It is naive to say that a world
power is by definition "imperialist" if it is capitalist and "altruistic"
if it is socialist. The question is, Can there be a political order on the
world level without the initial triumph of socialism? Even if one
believes that such a revolution should occur first, there may not be
enough time for the world to realize this aim, and, independent of
whether the revolution against capitalist structures occurs, the need
for a world system of law and order still exists, for economic rivalry
and war are just as likely to develop between communist states as
between other social systems.

In my judgment, a considerable part of the Marxist critique is
mistaken. The great issue is whether the world shall become democratic or totalitarian. Socialist societies that are undemocratic or
totalitarian are as unresponsive to the needs of the people as are
rapacious monopoly capitalist societies. The real questions plaguing
the world are of another sort. Yet because of a Marxist ideological

religion on one side, and an inordinate suspicion and fear of communist revolution on the other, a rigid paranoia has set in, preventing our working together to create a better community for all men.

What is at stake is not the usual communist-capitalist alternative, but the best answers we can achieve to these most urgent questions:

(1) *How can the world develop its economic resources, eliminate poverty and disease, provide an adequate standard of living, and satisfy the basic life-needs of all human beings.*

There is no guarantee that socialist societies can outproduce capitalist societies. They have not been able to do so in food production, and the growth rates of many capitalist states—Japan, Germany and Brazil, for example—have exceeded those of communist states. To say that communism must overtake capitalism may be wishful thinking, following from an uncritical, religious faith in the dialectic. In 1913, Czarist Russia was the fifth country in the world in global production; in annual percentage increase it was growing faster than England, Germany, or France, and, except for two five-year periods (1885 to 1889 and 1901 to 1906) its rate of industrial increase was faster than that of the United States. It was only twentieth in per capita production. This rate of growth has continued until now Russia is second in the world in global production. But it is still twentieth in the world in per capita production. The balance between consumers' goods and producers' goods was much better in the closing years of Nicholas II than it has been ever since. In Russia in 1966-67 it took 46 minutes of labor time to earn a kilo of flour, in the United States 6 minutes, and in England 10. The working time for a kilo of beef was 222 minutes for Russia, 83 for England, and 45 for the United States.

The strongest argument for a free economy is that it outproduces and is more efficient than a bureaucratic, centrally managed one. Ideology, therefore, should not be permitted to outmaneuver productivity. On paper, socialism many appear more just and humane than capitalism, yet for the citizen in the last analysis it is *praxis* that counts. And if the energies of quasi-capialist society can provide for maximum economic growth and prosperity, then it has a clear advantage, particularly for those portions of the globe where economic development is desperately needed. It may be that the open secret of capitalist success is that it allows for incentive, innovation, creativity;

not having to clear every one of its moves with centralized controllers, it can permit the free play of experiment and ingenuity. Can socialist systems free individual innovation and achieve high productivity? It is a major question and mere Marxist piety is no substitute for an answer. The other major question is whether the capitalist system can be responsive to the wider needs of the people.

(2) *Whatever the economic system, how is it possible to allocate resources and develop an investment strategy that will not only increase productivity, but avoid waste of economic resources, environmental pollution, and other spoilage?*

Among the vices of capitalist enterprise are that in seeking profits it often adulterates the product and ignores the possibly dangerous effects; that in excessive competition there is often great waste; that monopolistic industries tend to fix prices, to develop mechanisms for contrived obsolescence; overemphasize growth which is deemed necessary to keep up the rate of profit; and underemphasize the long-range consequences. Should society build ten million automobiles instead of ten million hi-fi sets? Should life be measured by quantitative or qualitative standards? Should industry be permitted to pollute our streams and air in order to turn a quick profit? Should it be allowed to exhaust our natural gas and oil resources?

Defenders of the capitalist mode of production argue that in the last analysis it is the consumer who is king, that economic decisions are made by him rather than by a bureaucracy, that bureaucratic societies are just as capable of waste as competitive societies, that the goods produced may be shoddier than under capitalism, and that production norms, replacing the profit motive, are more prone to measure quantity rather than quality. Lake Bakal is becoming as polluted as Lake Erie, and the smoke and soot in Zagreb appear to be as strong as in London. Technocratic managers in both capitalist and socialist societies guide productive forces and have a similar deleterious impact upon ecology. The point is that the "space-ship earth" has a finite number of resources; and the mad haste to exploit them, whether for profit or production norms, whether by capitalist or socialist industries, must be questioned. It is urgent that we regulate trade and the exploitation of natural resources, and regulate them internationally.

Who can most rationally regulate the development of the world's

natural resources, and limit the damaging environmental consequences of excessive production and consumption? Who can ensure
that the runaway population growth can be curtailed and begin to
approach the zero level? Who can see to it that the controls will be
consonant with individual freedom, will be voluntary, and based
upon education rather than compulsion?

By extrapolating from current growth rates, we can estimate that
by the year 2000 the world's economy will expand yearly output
enormously. If present rates of production continue, the world will
consume 1,700 million short tons of steel, 60 billion barrels of crude
petroleum, 600 short tons of coal, 340 million short tons of meat,
110 million motor vehicles, and fly 15 billion passenger-miles in
civil aviation. It is now recognized that, given the energy shortages,
these rates must be scaled down. In addition, if present population
growth rates continue, the world population will approximately
double by the year 2000, and may even reach 15 billion by the year
2020. Even though zero population growth is close at hand in the
United States, it is not in the rest of the world.

What will runaway growth do to natural resources and to the
ecology? What will it do to the quality of life? Will we so strain our
limited resources that at some point we will reach an impassable
economic barrier? The world is rapidly approaching a global economic problem of such mammoth proportions that no nation by itself
can resolve it. Refusal to face up to the problem will only mean
risking greater ecological and economic disaster. Whether the underdeveloped countries will ever be able to catch up with the developed
nations, and whether, if they do, the rate of industrial production will
mean utter depletion of natural resources, the death of marine and
wild life, is a momentous issue. The only alternative is for the world
to adopt a global strategy for rational economic planning, to permit
a maximum of freedom both for individuals and nations, but to lay
down guidelines. Danish fishermen, for example, should not be
permitted to exceed a certain level of salmon catch, so as not to
endanger the species; Russian whalers should be restricted in the
number of whales they may kill, Canadian sealers in the numbers
of seals; and U.S. garbage vessels should be prevented from dumping
raw sewage in the ocean. The mad depletion of oil reserves, the
elimination of forests, the pollution of the atmosphere, cannot con-

tinue. To build an Aswan dam may destroy the delta of the Nile and the fresh fish of the Mediterranean; to exploit the north shore of Alaska or to dam the fresh waters of the Arctic may affect the balance of the oceans. For one nation to decide not to build a supersonic transport plane for ecological reasons makes no sense if others do not act likewise. The President of the United States or the Secretary of the Communist Party of the USSR cannot be permitted to adopt a budget or economic plan without some reference to its impact on the rest of the world.

The issue, then, is not *whether* to adopt a world strategy of economic development and ecological preservation, but *when it will be forced upon us.* We are reaching a point when no one government can decide whether to encourage the birth rate or to make contraceptive knowledge freely available. The survival of our species is at stake. Population is a global issue, not a matter for individual men or nations.

I am not talking about rigid centralized or authoritarian planning. That, I think, is apt to restrict initiative. What I have in mind is coordinated planning, advisory boards, international consultation. This is already happening in a sense, for the international monetary system is increasingly a result of negotiation and bargaining by a council of the ministers of major capitalist nations. We need to extend this process on a global scale and apply it to the allocation and exploitation of natural resources, a task that must be entrusted to a world body.

(3) *Which of the economic systems is most democratically free and responsive to the needs and interests of people and to the community?*

A capitalist society needs to make corporate powers responsive to the needs of the community. The profit incentive must be subsumed under the public good. As one example, although strip mining may be a cheap and profitable way of extracting metals, it leads to dreadful ecological and aesthetic damage, and must be regulated; a corporation must be judged by its effect upon the greater community.

In my discussion of participatory democracy I said that the need within organizations is for the people in them to distribute responsibility with the aim of developing social concern. We must also bring in consumers and have public members representing wider interests on boards of directors. Since both management and labor have had occasion to ignore the public interest—unions can be as self-seeking as stockholders—it is necessary for such institutions to become socially responsible. The TVA, the New York Port Authority which operates the airports and bridges in the greater New York City area, and NET (educational television) are quasi-public corporations operating with private initiative and existing for public purposes.

Regulatory measures for corporations may achieve some of the aims of socialism without the nationalization of all the means of production. The productive capacity of the U.S. economic system is extraordinary. The gross national product, which has passed well beyond one trillion dollars, may very well treble by the year 2000, if present trends continue. Socialist recommendations that the United States radically shift its economic structure sound like pleas to kill an economy that lays a golden egg for the promise of a social system that has not as yet been able to satisfy the needs of its people, nor to provide democracy or freedom. It is only if and when the socialist mode of production can ensure productivity *and* guarantee freedom for its citizens, that it would be time to consider a change.

I do not believe the decisive issue of our time to be the need to destroy classes, as Marx thought. The needs are for excessive economic power to be curbed by progressive taxation and regulation, for society to be opened up by equality of opportunity, for elites to be made responsive to criticism and democratic control. The need is not to destroy leadership, but to apply its talent as far as possible for the good of society.

In certain contexts some form of socialism is clearly the most effective method of social and economic development, particularly where there is an entrenched and intransigent class of wealthy families who are selfishly interested in their aggrandizement rather than the public good. Where there is not a large amount of working capital, an entrepreneurial group, nor a high level of education, it is essential that the state stimulate and develop trade and industry. Thus in some areas socialism appears to be the best path to economic change; in other cases, a mixed economic system is more efficacious. In France, the automobile, aviation, and railway companies are nationalized; in Sweden and other Scandinavian countries, other industries are owned by the public sector. Whether it is adopted wholly or partially, however, socialization must permit democratic regulation and initiative. The danger in socialist economies has been over-bureaucratization and over-centralized planning, and most dangerous, the monopoly by one party of political and economic power, destroying individual freedom. Only a thoroughly democratic and decentralized socialism could begin to fulfill the needs of its people.

(4) *How close the gap between the have and have-not nations?*

The overriding issue for the remainder of the 20th century is likely to be caused by the disparity between the developed and under-developed nations—between the nations enjoying unprecedented affluence and prosperity (which now includes the oil-rich Arab states), and the majority of mankind who remain in poor and over-populated lands. If the underdeveloped countries cannot meet their expectations, the result is bound to be explosive. The wealthy nations have an obligation to increase the production of the rest of the world. Yet all forecasts suggest that the disparity in wealth and income is increasing; the great hopes for narrowing the gap are not being fulfilled. It is inescapable that only world government and global economic development can hope to resolve this problem. The great powers today grant aid to national governments on a bilateral basis; if the aid fails to increase their own power or influence, it is diminished or cut off. The new humanist morality must take as its first priority the redistribution of income on a world-wide basis. On the other hand economic game plans based primarily upon a redistribution of income are never adequate by themselves. The need is to redirect productivity, quantitatively and qualitatively. We should not seek to divide a limited pie but to increase its size; however, we must be concerned not simply with the increase of gross national product, but with the improvement of the quality of life. It is not who owns or controls the means of production that matters as much as how production is stimulated and used. Yet the hope of mankind does not depend simply upon changing our institutions, but upon developing new forms of technology. It is not merely what we invent that counts, but the uses to which we put our inventions. On this hinges not merely the quality of life, but life itself.

THE PROMISE OF TECHNOLOGY

Any account of history that claims to be adequate must emphasize the role of technology. It was largely by means of technological discovery and invention that man was able to improve upon his primitive habitat, transform his society and, indeed, his globe and then finally lift himself into space. If one were to write a scenario for the future of man, technology would be the key. Man may be overwhelmed by technological blight or attain unparalleled heights of achievement and happiness.

Science is a method of inquiry, with rigorous criteria for determining the validity of its hypotheses. Its hypotheses are (1) based upon and verified by factual data and experiment, (2) judged by their internal logical relationships, and (3) tested by their consequences in practice. The scientific method thus involves a union of empiricism and rationalism on the one hand and pragmatism on the other, which enables us to resolve problems encountered in the world of experience.

In the theoretical sciences and research we investigate causes, seeking to explain how and why things behave the way they do. Causal theories and laws are treated as hypotheses; they are modified in the course of inquiry by their effectiveness in relating to previously confirmed hypotheses, by their internal consistency, and by how they account for newly uncovered facts. In basic research we develop conceptual models that are vital in helping to create new world views and in extending our basic understanding of nature and of man.

The changes in our theoretical conceptions have had profound impact upon our beliefs, attitudes, and values. The Aristotelian system was a comprehensive theoretical account of the universe in terms of teleological categories; it summed up the knowledge of the ancient world and was adopted by the medieval world to provide a framework for the Judaic-Christian faith. The Copernican-Newtonian world-view abandoned the Aristotelian doctrine of final causes and overthrew the theological universe; all hypotheses were to be tested by experiment and mathematics. The modern scientific view broadened our perspective of the universe and minimized man's place within it. The earth was no longer the center of the universe; all events were seen to operate in terms of causal laws. In the 19th century, Darwinian evolutionary theories overthrew the classical philosophical-theological view of man, and naturalized and biologized his behavior. This had a fundamental effect upon his moral, religious, and philosophical beliefs. In the 20th century, the revolution in the behavioral and social sciences has again enlarged and modified man's conception of himself and his universe, contributing further to the impact of science on our values, which are of course intimately related to what we think we are and how we think we fit into nature. The cumulative effect of the scientific enterprise has been to free man from previous mythological-theological-metaphysical views of nature, and to liberate and naturalize his values; it has forced man to think critically about what he is and what he ought to be; and it has been powerful in demythologizing our dreams, debunking our illusions, shattering our dogmas. It has bolstered our autonomy and independence, permitting us to increase our control of our destinies. By understanding nature, man is able to use it as far as he can to fulfill his own purposes. Science is human power at its height; it grows out of man's intellect, it gives vent to his courage, and it feeds his audacity. But it is not only an intellectual affair or a source of value; it unsettles objects, it intervenes in nature, it engenders new worlds. Scientific theory insofar as it is related to technology is practical, dynamic, instrumental. Man is a tool-maker and tool-user. From the earliest hunters and fishermen, from the first use of fire, from the invention of the wheel and the arrow, from the beginnings of agriculture and elementary industry, man has employed his powers of reflection to change the world by way of arts and crafts through the manipulation of tools. It is science preeminently that provides man with instruments of utility and power: and so long as he continues to investigate causes and consequences, man will construct daringly and achieve innovations which will alter his behavior in turn. Science is man attempting to fathom the world; technology is his effort to change it to suit his purposes and fulfill his needs.

The present juncture at which Promethean man stands is in large measure a result of the science and technology which have transformed his universe. Because of his attainments man now stands poised between threat and promise.

Threats to Humankind

If invention gives us new powers, its consequences are often unpredictable. The emergence of new technologies in agricultural production—the harvest, the grinding of seeds to make flour and bread —contributed to a new mode of society, giving stability and tranquility to what had otherwise been a nomadic hunting existence, and radically transforming the natural terrain. Similarly, the growth of commerce and industry threw man into an urban environment and made possible a new form of civilized life. Both the pastoral and urban modes of existence led, however, to unforeseen problems: An agricultural technology made possible the development of large imperial armies in the ancient world and an industrial technology multiplied the means of destruction. The science of ballistics led to the weaponry of gunshot and cannon, nuclear physics and bio-chemistry to more sophisticated and deadly weapons of mass destruction. Though an urban civilization liberated man from dependence upon hunting, it cast him into an artificial environment which drastically altered the course of his existence.

As technology resulted in new breakthroughs its transforming effect became even greater. The ocean-going vessel opened up new continents and made world-wide communication possible; through these continents the locomotive forged, creating new networks for transportation. The automobile took man more readily into and out of the city, into and out of the suburbs and countryside and changed the city into a center of pollution and congestion. Airplane travel put Peking, Rome and Chicago within easy reach of each other; instantaneous radio, television, telephone, and satellite communication have virtually nullified distance. Medical technology has mitigated human suffering by reducing pain and lowering the death rate. Agricultural technology has made possible increases both in population and food production, which in turn have stimulated the rate of population expansion to leap ahead still further.

In the 18th and 19th centuries, perhaps anticipating some of these events, man believed that progress was continuous and that by means of science he could eventually solve the problems of life. It was not so easy to foresee the dangers inherent in leaps forward in technology, among them urban blight, atomic radiation, ecological destruction, excessive population. And now many people ask nostalgically whether limits should not be placed upon scientific research and invention. We were better off, they insist, when we enjoyed simpler modes of existence, before the automobile and airplane, before plastics, and detergents, and napalm. Here we find a plea to restore some of the romance of an earlier, less complicated life. The counterculture's return to the commune is an effort to save the qualities of immediate experience in nature, to find new purpose in the good life, which is increasingly difficult for contemporary man. It is a vision that is profoundly humane and moving; it is a call from the wild, out of man's deepest primeval past.

That our increasingly sophisticated technology has had bad effects is obvious, but it is also obvious that we cannot stop the technological clock, nor wind it back. Our problem is not technology *per se* but its misuse. We must concentrate on overcoming the dangers that accrue with new devices, and try to guard against their future misapplications. The counter-technological culture has hammered the point home: Technology does not exist for itself but for the good of mankind. The lesson is clear. We need to humanize our technology, to master its course, but we also need to invent new technological systems to correct the defects of the old.

Mankind always exists in suspended existential option. Today, we recognize that we can by the abuse of our technological prowess cause our own destruction. On the other hand, the religious-mystical-poetic tendencies in man can overwhelm him. He can lose the courage to be; he can cower in fear and trembling. It has happened before in the history of man. After the age of Greece and Rome, when man had attained new heights of philosophical and artistic glory, life was beset by a religious revival in which a civilization was destroyed and overrun by barbarism and primitiveness. Each new generation must learn and cherish the history of the race, but there is no guarantee of that. A new mood of anti-scientific fervor carried to fanatical extremes may engulf us. The consequences in suffering would be incalculable.

As we approach the 21st century, anyone who extrapolates from the statistical charts can only be appalled. Philip M. Hauser, writing on population, says: "Given the present outlook, only the faithful who believe in miracles from heaven, the optimistic who anticipate superwonders from science, the parochial fortunate who think they can continue to exist on islands of affluence in a sea of world poverty, and the naive who anticipate nothing, can look to the future with equanimity."[1]

Every sort of doomsday prophecy has been uttered. It is not mere fashion or cliché. Much of it is related to reality. Man can destroy himself utterly in war, or he may so poison his atmosphere that life on earth would be rendered impossible. An uncontrolled population can impoverish mankind. These scenarios are all possible for our future and we should look at them without illusions. The human species can become extinct. Only a fanatic will be content to believe that nature has a special place for man or that a divine being will protect us from self-destruction. The only guarantee that we have in the future as in the past is ourselves.

There are trends and directions in history; given knowledge of historical conditions, we often can predict what will occur in the future, but we cannot do so infallibly. There are only probabilities. We cannot predict the unexpected, the contingent, the accidental. There is always the possibility of a new crisis becoming a new turning point, directing tendencies in an unexpected way. Machiavelli claimed in *The Prince* that human affairs are ruled by *fortuna* and *virtù*, by chance and by men. One cannot say whether some unexpected event, some crisis or bizarre occurrence, will not intervene to disrupt the course of human destiny. Because of this, how man responds to the challenges of his physical and social environment is decisive. The career of the human species is a product of its art. Will man master blind forces by means of rational control? Can he use his technology to bend the future as he wishes?

The Promise of Technology

There is a new adventure awaiting mankind and it may be more exciting than anything we have experienced until now. What our future will be depends in part upon the images that we create. We must

[1] *Toward the Year 2018,* ed. by the Foreign Policy Assn., N. Y., Cowles Education Corporation, 1968, p. vii.

articulate new possible futures for mankind. We must be receptive to imaginative alternatives and be willing to entertain new conceptual models of life.

At the beginning of this century few imagined how our lives would be transformed by the automobile, aviation, the telephone, motion pictures, radio, television. In 1939 few were aware of the impending uses of atomic energy, jet propulsion, antibiotics, organ transplants, space travel, radar, computer technology, the transistor—all now taken for granted. Today there are significant new discoveries in the sciences that await application. The scale and tempo of technological development are accelerating. A new idea emerges, a possible application is suggested, it is experimentally implemented, if the experiment is successful mass production begins—all at an increasingly rapid pace. We can no longer simply look ahead five or ten years. We must now consider generations, possibly centuries. We need to see where we are going so that we can plan to get there. Marx and Engels are important figures in the modern world not because of their specific ideological theories, but because they were concerned with understanding trends in history and by that knowledge to try to improve the lot of man. Our forecasting today must endeavor by every means to become more accurate. No one can anticipate with any certainty the future discoveries of science, but lack of complete certainty notwithstanding, some forecasting of direction is possible. We have clues to inventions that are within the range of calculated projections; though some seem remote they need to be discussed for they are possible.

Looking ahead to the 21st century we may list four areas in which some of the most significant developments are likely to occur. What they portend cannot now be fully anticipated. That they will have a revolutionary impact seems obvious:

(1) *Increased control over nature.*   It is likely that man will enormously expand his ability to modify the environment. Environmental change is not new. To speak of the "balance of nature" in mystical terms as if this were some hidden or sacred wisdom that cannot be tampered with is nonsense. We have been changing nature for thousands of years. The development of agriculture altered the balance; it entailed cutting down trees, clearing fields, damming streams, irrigating lands, replanting new trees, vegetables, plants and

domesticating and raising herds of cattle. Today the Israelis illustrate this by turning arid and rocky desert into lush green farmlands. We should not retreat from the advantages of changing our environment. We must be more careful, and morally so, to change it so as to avoid negative results. Faced with seemingly irreparable ecological damage, we can create entirely new environments, self-contained atmospheres; we can control weather and crown cities with protective domes. We can literally bend the environment to suit our needs. Of course we all want to preserve some of the original primitive areas of the world but the earth is ours and, within measurable limits, we can supply our needs by humane restructuring. The future of man must involve the creation of new and better environments. We need to develop urban and ecological planning on a large scale, to convert urban blight and slums into centers of joy and delight. We can only speculate on the forms they will take but that they will involve daring departures is certain.

We will also extend our energy resources. The history of civilization from animal and human manual labor to the lever, the pulley, and the windmill, from water, steam and fossil fuels to nuclear power, can be measured by our ability to transform energy into work. It is now clear that our major sources of energy—coal, natural gas, and oil—will some day be depleted. Accordingly, new sources will be discovered, including solar energy and a safe, efficient way of utilizing nuclear power. The bounty to civilization from such uses will be enormous.

Science-fiction writing of the past has been concerned with improved communication and travel, with a whole new world of technological gadgets, automata, computers, and robots—and much of it that seemed impossible has actually come to pass. As always, man will discover and create new materials and put them to new uses, for his comfort, pleasure and creative activity. While the realization of such a good life can hardly be guaranteed to eliminate pain or suffering or failure, it will immeasurably enhance the conditions of life. Man is a creature of nature, but living in society he can summon up in his imagination a world and go on to build it, as an extension of himself, ministering to his needs yet eventually modifying his nature. He has already transcended some of his limits, and by bringing into being something new, by converting his ideals into reality, he frees himself from acceptance of his surroundings and shapes his world as he wants it.

(2)   *Control of human behavior.*   We will extend our control not only over nature and forces outside our body, but over ourselves. There are impending breakthroughs in the behavioral sciences that will provide us with enormous power to understand how and why we act as we do and how we can control or change our behavior. The methods nearest at hand are those of operant conditioning and reinforcement in behavioral psychology (B. F. Skinner), and of electrical, chemical, and thermal stimulation of the brain.[2] A computer technology will help us map out the structure of the brain in order to understand how it functions. It is now conceivable that drugs can be developed to expand intelligence and memory, to stimulate analytic ability and insight, to reform personality and character. The implantation of electrodes in the brains of primates and humans already enables us to control behavior, to influence emotional states, to stimulate cognitive thought and perceptual images. There will be great efforts to plan and design the socio-cultural environment, not only to benefit man's soma, but the conditions of the environment in which he operates. The great moral issue is whether we can maintain a libertarian ethic of freedom and democracy. The temptations to create utopias beyond the individual's control will be great and must be rendered impossible. It is possible to use computers and cybernetic machines as extensions of our brain. Thus the promise of the future contains the seed of threat. The morality of a humane vision must keep watch over every negative element.

(3)   *The genetic control of evolution.*   A most provocative possibility emerges from the increased power of man to control the course of his evolution. We already influence the evolutionary process by social mechanisms that regulate survival and reproduction. Much of this has been unplanned and unconscious, but there are developments now that will give us the power to intervene consciously in the basic course of life, to eliminate genetic defects, to discover, abort or correct retarded or deformed fetuses, to get rid of diabetes, epilepsy, and other disabling diseases. It is virtually possible now to

[2] See José M. R. Delgado, "Psychocivilized Direction of Behavior," *The Humanist*, March/April 1972.

select the sex of the unborn child, even to eliminate the need for the usual methods of sexual reproduction. Experimental scientists may be able to clone individuals, that is, to duplicate individuals by asexual means, and also to create new forms of artificial life. It is possible for us to inseminate eggs artificially and to breed fetuses in vitro—that is, outside the womb of the mother. Perhaps it will be possible to transcend the differences between the sexes. Since the humans of the future will no longer need to be hunters, farmers, industrial workers, or even reproducers, distinctions in sexual role need not be as sharp. If we discover that in interplanetary space we will need additional organs, it may be possible to add them. By means of bio-genetic engineering we may also be able to overcome genetic differences in race. The science of eugenics will be able to change man himself, regardless of his environment or his society.

Related to this is the promise of extending life far beyond its present limits. If we can control accident and disease, why not extend the life-span for most people to 100 or 120 years? Although there is a genetically-based aging process in each species, some biologists have nevertheless speculated that we may be able to extend life much further. We can transplant organs and add artificial mechanisms to create cyborgs, equipped with brains and other vital organs, but little else. If life can be extended, one may speculate on how it can be enriched so that a predominantly gerontological race can find happiness and well-being? All these developments will no doubt lead to great moral problems. Our morality is increasingly feeling the effect of new technologies; it needs constantly to be reconsidered.

(4) *The colonizing of space.* In the present age for the first time we are able to break out of earth's gravity and to travel in space. In less than a decade technological advances made possible the incredible leap from the first Sputnik to landing on the moon.

The ability to travel in space, like the use of fire, the invention of the wheel, the development of language, doubtless signals a crucial turning point in the history of mankind. As we advance in interplanetary and interstellar travel, we may be able to find new places to live. The remote dream of colonizing other planets may become possible—a breathtaking vision which may embrace the necessity of genetic engineering of major proportions. Even now questions about the kinds of hibernation or suspended animation which would be necessary to sustain us on the long voyage through outer space are being asked by scientists. Our future may again become primarily nomadic: rootless, mobile, exploring the unknown. Perhaps our greatest question is whether man will encounter other forms of life and what he will learn about his place in the universe. Humanism takes man as the center of concern, but if we were to meet other forms of life, other forms of intelligence, other civilizations, this would have a transforming effect upon our sense of who we are and where we are to go—upon all our concepts and values.

Space travel is primarily a tribute to scientific humanism. Man, of all the animals on this planet, has been able to leap beyond it by the use of his intelligence and scientific skill. The age of space has already opened up new and uncharted areas. It has immediate and dramatic implications for man's life on earth. When our globe is viewed from the wider perspective of space, man's racial, nationalistic, religious, ethnic, and class antagonisms hardly seem meaningful. Accordingly, in the age of space our chief commitment is to the party of humankind, for all humans are truly part of one system.

Our ability to change our environment, to engage in dramatic behavioral and genetic control, and to travel in space will no doubt accentuate the crisis in morality that we are undergoing today. Concomitant with each step in the scientific technological advance there are reverberations in our moral values; the established patterns of one generation become more quickly than ever outmoded in the next. The age of space demonstrates finally the persistent need to engage in rational moral and social reconstruction.

IN SUMMATION

The crucial question for mankind in the future is whether we will be willing and able to take the new departures available. Can we use our Promethean talents to the fullest? Can we employ humanely the new powers we will possess to restructure radically the nature of human beings? As I have stated, egalitarian-environmentalists have recognized the role of society in determining what man can be; and they have pointed to the need for fundamental changes in social structures if we are to achieve our ideals. But, as I have argued in this book, they have been mistaken in stressing one-factor theories and in sanctifying them as the means of human salvation. Granted that to achieve further progress mankind needs to create one world and to plan rationally for its social and economic development; we must also encourage the imminent possibilities bestowed upon us by technology. The sciences now indicate that if man is to ennoble his future, he must recognize the opportunities available not only in social or psychological change but in biological and chemical change as well. We must learn how to restructure our genetic natures, which heretofore have limited us.

The moral center of the question is in our choices of how we wish to change and what we want to become. Sex, individuality, love, hate, and death are all inherent in the human condition. The elements of unpredictability of the bizarre and the unique, of success and tragedy, all play shifting roles in the human drama. Man now possesses the gifts and powers to overcome some of the natural forces that have limited him, but only if he can exercise the moral discipline to take his own destiny as far as he can into his hands.

I do not mean to exaggerate our capabilities. We should not be carried away wishfully by the lure of the possible, nor believe that it can easily become the actual. In the nature of things, we are still frail animals, and though capable of creating wonders, we are still prone to error, limited in power, finite in an infinite universe. Although we may tap new sources of energy, there are doubtless powers which we must recognize and appreciate as beyond our control. There is a serene unfathomableness in the universe, far greater than man. We are insignificant by the measure of eternity.

Man can be overpowered by his sense of the boundless universe. He can be crushed by a final realization of the tragic aspects of human existence. In the contest between man and the universe, in the last analysis, it is man whose will must yield; and it is he, who will finally cave in, not the universe. Out, alone, in breathtaking space, his impotence and insignificance may be too much for him to bear. A new religious awakening and a new sense of awe and piety may again descend upon him. The stress of the tempo of change in the post-modern technological world may be too much for the human system. Man may again retreat in a massive expression of failure of nerve. This has happened before in human history, and may repeat itself.

Every reader of this book has heard and read of all sorts of grim futures that doomsayers have imagined for the human species: nuclear disaster, totalitarian thought control, the emergence of a new dark age. Because they exploit man's fears, such apocalyptic visions have always threatened to come true, and fanaticisms of one kind or another have therefore offered illusory refuge. We have seen how in abandoning theism, men have been all too prone to seize upon other religious ideologies, Marxism among them. When that has finally been dismantled by bitter experience, men may seek to cling to new faiths, or old faiths by new names, that they imagine will sustain them.

A great lesson of history is that mankind needs to reject facile solutions, easy promises of salvation, whether religious or ideological. The present-day controversies among the isms, capitalism, liberalism, communism, seem—in the light of our desires and capacities—irrelevant. They deflect us from the ultimate problems we must consider *now,* when our means of survival and our means of destruction have become equally powerful. The only option for man is to think about his future not in traditional ideological terms but radically and rationally in terms of his creative potentialities.

The challenge in every age is the existential dilemma: Is life worth living? man still cries out. What does it mean? How do we fit into the universe? Do we have a place in it?

Man can learn to recognize the universe for what it is. He can live without illusion. He can discard the myths imposed upon him in his infancy, and realize that utopia is always a matter of increasing degree, that by discovering the sources of enrichment and joy, he will find that the good life is truly possible—an interesting, exciting, inspiring adventure. If he is realistic he will know that he sometimes will fail, but that he will often succeed. Learning that he cannot suppress change, he may learn to manage, indeed to encourage it when he sees how to use it for human betterment.

A continuing moral revolution accompanying technological change will no doubt accelerate the stresses involved in discovering new values and meanings in our existence. It will have continuing repercussions—in our social life, in our educational system, the nature of marriage and the family, political and economic institutions.

Our basic problem is moral: to survive and to live well, and to be a conscious member of the family of man, aware that we are all linked in humanity, and thus able to utilize the instruments of science, technology, and the arts of society for universally worthwhile purposes.

In this approach to the future, the qualities that man needs to foster if he is to survive are critical intelligence, compassion, and courage—qualities he should never be willing to barter for vain promises. Man, the primate with the enlarged cerebral cortex and the ability to respond to symbols and use language, needs critical intelligence for his survival, his needs and functions, and his exploration of new forms of his life-adventure. But, living in community, he needs to develop compassion for his fellow beings. He needs to be constantly aware that all humans live and suffer together, and that by sharing our experiences of joy, of sorrow, and hope, we give new meaning to life. The moral point of view is a prerequisite for human survival.

And man needs to cultivate his courage and persistence to explore the universe and mold the world to his desire, or that small portion of it that he occupies, to withstand inevitable, difficult events, and by recognizing the tragic elements, not to be unwittingly defeated by them.

These are high marks of human greatness, the excellencies that a humanism of freedom appropriate to the present human condition needs to nourish. That reason, empathy, and independence should be assiduously cultivated as cherished virtues, if the destiny of man is not to be terminated abruptly, has become increasingly clear. It is now entirely possible for human life to enter a new age of promise and splendor. Whether it will do so will depend not upon conflicting faiths in God or utopias or ideologies in strife of opposition, but upon the resources of the human animal and whether or not he is realistic, creative and daring enough to stand up to new challenges and demands. The fullness of being is still within man's reach, with evidence on every hand that it can be fuller and more intense than any that has gone before. Whether we will be able to realize these potentialities cannot be determined beforehand. Our future is contingent and precarious, open and uncharted; and what it will be depends upon the decisions and actions that we will undertake. Whether our choices will spell wisdom or folly can only be told after the fact. If our choices are to be wise, then a precondition for human achievement is that we must not delude ourselves or be weighed down by a false religiosity of the spirit. If we will but give full vent to the highest within us—our intelligence, our capacity for compassion, our audacious spirit—we will be devoted to the only religion appropriate to mankind, that which takes the fulfillment of man's hopes by man himself as the center of his universe and his primary project.